ROBERT J. MOORE
AWARD-WINNING, BEST-SELLING AUTHOR

MAGNETIC

ENTREPRENEUR

Collaborate to Succeed

Legal Disclaimer

Connect with Magnetic Entrepreneur Inc.™
https://www.facebook.com/magneticentrepreneur
www.linkedin.com/in/magneticentrepreneur
E-Mail: magneticentrepreneur2017@gmail.com
Website: magnetic-entrepreneur.com

Dedication

This book is dedicated to all the courageous entrepreneurs
who take risks and are willing to face
all obstacles and overcome them.
You are the true magnetic ones.

COLLABORATE TO SUCCEED

ACKNOWLEDGEMENTS

First of all, I would like to thank amazing leaders like Les Brown, Raymond Aaron, Eric Thomas, Ted McGrath, Mel Robbins, The Ziglar Family, and Kyle Wilson and many more. Not only are they true Magnetic Entrepreneurs, but they freely share their knowledge with others. Without these mentors in my life, I wouldn't be where I am today.

This book would not be possible without the great contributions of the co-authors. They are real-life examples of people who started out sometimes with nothing and now are not only successful businesspeople but also experts in their own right.

Thank you for letting your entrepreneurial spirit shine through and encouraging others by sharing your stories and lessons learned. You are an inspiration to all who will read this book!

To *Les Brown*: You are an inspiration to us all. Your ground-breaking work is seen all over the world, and your expertise overall really benefits us all. Thank you for contributing your foreword to this book.

Finally, to you, the reader: No book comes alive until it is read. Thank you for investing in yourself and your future. You will never regret that.

Robert J. Moore

Founder of Magnetic Entrepreneur Inc.™

TABLE OF CONTENTS

Contents

FOREWORD

There is something in the air. Do you smell it? Maybe you can feel it? And if you are not careful, you can be infected by it. Infected by the wave of negativity, stinking thinking, self-doubt, and fear. Somehow or another, the virus can be highly contagious and lingers if you do not protect yourself from it. Now more than ever, it is imperative to change your mindset in order to change your life, protect yourself, and combat the virus. Negativity must die along with the parasite's low self-worth and toxic relationships.

No matter what, I am a firm believer in possibility thinking. It's Possible, and It's Not Over Until You Win are among my most famous and impactful quotes, but change cannot occur unless there is Hope.

This book, its content, and the brilliance of its authors poured their most professional and personal transparency within these pages. This masterpiece will inspire anyone to a healthier lifestyle, give your business that extra hidden awareness that you have overlooked.

More than 20 years ago, I heard the most feared words around the world, Les, you have cancer. What a slap in the face, I thought. Why me? I questioned. My life hit a low point. I was at the height of my career, I still had young children, and I felt robbed. Looking back, the cancer diagnosis was my hope for turning things around. As a 20-year cancer conqueror, my journey to getting well began with the fear of dying too soon. I listened to my doctors, and I listened more to positive messages and quotes. The thought of having cancer alone almost killed me. I made it a point to search for hope, survivors, and answers to beat cancer. I had to kill the bacteria of doubt in my mind.

For me, this book has cracked the secret code for success. It does not include waving a magic wand, clicking your heels three times, or throwing a penny into a wishing well. It is a formula requiring more than the typical 'concentrate on your health, goals, and thinking happy thoughts'; the authors present life-changing information and challenge us to focus on our mission with an incredible effort and sustained action over time in order to get maximized potential, which is changing the world!

There is a cure for this viral infection, and if the pages within this book are applied correctly, your wit, grit, and stamina will improve. You will find your confidence at an all-time high, and it will yield positive results. The method is equivalent to a modern-day Einstein strategy. Each contributor has their own proven track record for their own personal and professional achievements and are capable of adding value to your life.

From personal experience, perseverance, nerve, and discipline include some of the many requirements to help you reach your mountaintop and high places in life. As we know, ultimate success takes time.; maximized potential takes even longer, and oftentimes most people simply graze the surface of their true talents, and they are miserable.

Again, I must ask, How healthy are you? If you cannot honestly answer that question, I urge you to immediately turn to the next page quickly; let's get you healthy, empowered, and ready to become an agent of change for yourself, your community, and the world at large.

I once heard, Consult not your fears but your hopes and your dreams. Think not about your frustrations but about your unfulfilled potential. Concern yourself not with what you tried and failed in but with what it is still possible for you to do.

You are going to have to fight to reach your destination. We are collectively at the Turning Point, do not get left behind. Always remember, it's possible, There is Hope! It may get hard but do it hard. See you at the top.

Yours in greatness,
Les Brown
www.LesBrown.com

INTRODUCTION

Finding good partners is the key to success in anything:
in business, in marriage and, especially in investing.

– Robert Kiyosaki

Business has dramatically changed in the last twenty years. It is a whole new world out there where there is the opportunity for anyone to grow an amazing business that creates financial freedom. No longer is it only big businesses that make all the money. With the advent of the internet, a whole new environment has been created where anyone with the right skills and training can become successful.

That is where the magnetic entrepreneur comes in. Old-school business techniques no longer work, and just throwing money into television and print ads does not bring the results wanted.

Why?

People are hungry for more. They are tired of being treated like brainless, second-class citizens who mindlessly follow whatever advertising tells them to do. The internet has now given them endless choices on how and where they spend their money. They can do research and make decisions on companies without ever entering their doors. One bad review, from the right person, on the wrong site and their sales can drop dramatically.

Customers and clients are tired of the crap. They want to work with and buy from entrepreneurs and companies that they know, like, and trust. They want to be treated as if they matter. This is why being a magnetic entrepreneur is essential for success in today's world.

You Must Be More

What does it mean to be "magnetic"?

In the Merriam-Webster dictionary (www.merriam-webster.com/dictionary), it says:

"Possessing an extraordinary power or ability to attract."

Some people naturally have a magnetic personality that does help in business but, if you look at the wording, it also says "ability." That means that there is hope. It is not only naturally gifted people who can succeed; anyone who wants to learn how, can.

But …

You must be willing to become more. That is where most people get stuck. They want to stay the way that they are and reap the rewards of the wealthy. There is a reason why so few people attain it. There is a cost to be a successful entrepreneur: you must become someone you are not.

There are things that you are going to have to let go of, and there are things that you are going to have to master through practice. There is no easy road to prosperity. You must earn it.

What sort of things are you going to have to let go of?

➢ Fear in all forms

➢ Poverty Mindset

➢ Not Enough Mindset

➢ Laziness

➢ Perfectionism

➢ Self-Doubt

These are only a few to get you started. Two hindrances will hold you back from success: what goes on in your head and heart and the skills and actions you need to get to where you want to go. When you conquer these, success can't help but come to you.

What will you have to master?

Communication Skills

One thing that differentiates successful entrepreneurs from others is their ability to communicate effectively with everyone. They speak carefully and consider their words before they come out of their mouth.

Emotional Control

Things will go wrong in business. The one who overcomes is the one who can control their heart. They don't overreact or take it personally; they step back, take an honest look at the situation, and then come up with a plan to fix things. Which leads to …

Unending Learning

Profound achievers get that way because every roadblock is an opportunity to learn and become more. They recognize that there is a solution to every problem; they just have to figure out what it is.

Sales Skills

You can be an entrepreneur and not know how to sell. However, anything that you do, and you don't sell, is a hobby. You do it because you enjoy it, but you don't necessarily make money from it. In order to be financially successful, especially as a solopreneur, you must be able to sell, or you won't have a business at all; just something you are good at.

Relationship Building Skills

You must recognize that your business will be built upon the relationships that you make with prospects, leads, customers, clients and other entrepreneurs. Each one requires a different skill, and you must master them all. Does it seem overwhelming? Don't let it get to you. Becoming a magnetic entrepreneur is a process that happens over time. You don't learn and implement everything in a week.

That is where all the authors in this book come in. They have "been there" and "done that" and are sharing their knowledge with you. They know the shortcuts and pitfalls that we all experience and are sharing their stories so you can succeed faster than they did.

Each author is an expert who has been at the bottom and worked their way up. Each one had to overcome significant obstacles and become more than they ever could imagine. In the pages of this book, you will learn from them what it means to become a truly magnetic entrepreneur.

Are you ready for an incredible journey? Are you ready to be propelled forward? Then turn the page, and let's get started.

-Robert J Moore

THE POWER OF MASTERMINDS

Robert J Moore

Robert J. Moore stands at the forefront of the entrepreneurial world, a visionary who believes in the immense power of masterminds. We now delve into the extraordinary value that masterminds provide and how they can transform both your personal and professional life.

Throughout his illustrious career, Robert has hosted numerous events under his brand, Magnetic Entrepreneur. One such event was the prestigious Magnetic Entrepreneur Author Awards, where aspiring authors from all walks of life gathered to celebrate their literary achievements. It was here that Robert witnessed the magic of collaboration as authors shared their stories, exchanged ideas, and forged powerful connections that would propel their careers forward.

But it didn't stop there. Robert's insatiable thirst for pushing boundaries led him to organize the Magnetic Entrepreneur Guinness World Records Attempt. The event brought together entrepreneurs from around the globe, aiming to break records and leave a lasting impact on the world. This record-breaking endeavour showcased the unparalleled potential of a collective mindset, where individuals united to achieve the seemingly impossible.

Yet, it was through his high-end Mastermind program that Robert truly unleashed the transformative force of collaboration. With each passing year, the program evolved, drawing in students from diverse backgrounds, ranging from novices seeking guidance to seasoned experts searching for fresh perspectives. Robert's unique ability to tailor his teachings to the individual needs of his students set him apart as a mastermind in his own right.

Through his program, Robert imparted the very techniques and strategies that he employed daily in his own thriving business. His philosophy was simple yet profound: by sharing his high-performance secrets, he aimed to empower his clients to duplicate his success in half the time. For Robert, every business, regardless of its size or industry, deserved to flourish and reach new heights.

The impact of Robert's work and his Magnetic Entrepreneur Inc. extended far beyond the entrepreneurial realm. His expertise had caught the attention of renowned publications like Forbes and Disrupt Magazines, propelling him into the limelight as a seasoned professional. Such recognition brought him great pride, but it was the lives he touched and transformed that truly fueled his passion.

Robert's achievements didn't stop at business accolades. He had achieved something extraordinary—twice. Robert was the proud recipient of an honourary doctorate degree, a testament to his unwavering dedication and indomitable spirit. His life's work had left an indelible mark, and through Magnetic Entrepreneur Inc., he continued to inspire, motivate, and uplift others to unleash their fullest potential.

As we embark on this journey through the phases of Robert J Moore's life, prepare to be captivated by his unwavering commitment to masterminds and the extraordinary impact they can have. With each turn of the page, we'll delve deeper into the world he has crafted — a world where dreams are realized, boundaries are shattered, and success becomes an inevitable outcome.

The Genesis of Magnetic Entrepreneur Inc.

The birth of Magnetic Entrepreneur Inc. was a testament to Robert J Moore's unyielding passion for empowering aspiring entrepreneurs and business owners. In this segment, we delve into the origins of this remarkable organization and the driving force behind its creation.

Robert's journey began long before the inception of Magnetic Entrepreneur Inc. It was a culmination of his own experiences, triumphs, and tribulations that led him to recognize the profound need for a platform that nurtured and supported individuals on their entrepreneurial path.

As a young man, Robert had always possessed an insatiable curiosity and a hunger for knowledge. His voracious appetite for learning propelled him to devour books, attend seminars, and seek out mentors who could guide him along his own entrepreneurial journey. He recognized the immense value in surrounding himself with like-minded individuals who shared his ambition and drive.

It was during this time that Robert discovered the power of collaboration and the concept of masterminds. He witnessed firsthand the exponential growth that could be achieved when brilliant minds united, shared their knowledge, and supported one another. The seeds of Magnetic Entrepreneur Inc. were sown in his mind.

Driven by a desire to create a transformative platform, Robert embarked on a mission to establish an organization that would serve as a beacon of inspiration, education, and community for entrepreneurs worldwide. With unwavering determination and a vision burning brightly within him, Magnetic Entrepreneur Inc. was brought to life.

The early days were filled with countless challenges and obstacles, but Robert's unshakable belief in his purpose propelled him forward. He knew that his mission was to provide aspiring entrepreneurs with the tools, resources, and support they needed to thrive.

Magnetic Entrepreneur Inc. soon became a sanctuary where dreams were nurtured, ideas were cultivated, and businesses were elevated to new heights. Through a carefully curated selection of programs, events, and mentorship opportunities, Robert and his team fostered an environment that encouraged innovation, collaboration, and personal growth.

The success stories began pouring in as entrepreneurs who had once struggled to find their footing discovered newfound clarity and direction. Through Magnetic Entrepreneur TV, a platform dedicated to sharing inspiring stories and expert insights, Robert amplified the voices of those who had overcome challenges and achieved remarkable success.

The impact of Magnetic Entrepreneur Inc. extended far beyond mere financial gains. It was a movement, a catalyst for change in the lives of countless individuals. Through business coaching and mentorship, Robert instilled the necessary skills and mindset shifts that empowered his clients to navigate the ever-evolving landscape of entrepreneurship with confidence and resilience.

The world took notice of Robert's remarkable achievements, and the accolades began to pour in. His ground-breaking work, coupled with his unwavering commitment to his clients' success, earned him international recognition as a best-selling author, speaker, and thought leader.

But for Robert, the true measure of success was not found in the awards and accolades. It was in the stories of individuals whose lives had been transformed through their association with Magnetic Entrepreneur Inc. It was in the newfound sense of purpose, fulfillment, and abundance that his clients now embraced.

As we journey further into the chapters of Robert J. Moore's extraordinary life, prepare to be captivated by the stories of triumph, resilience, and the unwavering spirit that propelled Magnetic Entrepreneur Inc. to the forefront of the entrepreneurial landscape. Together, we shall explore the transformative power of education, mentorship, and community in shaping the destiny of those who dare to dream.

The Magnetic Entrepreneur Manifesto

Next, we delve into the incredible journey of Robert J. Moore, the visionary behind Magnetic Entrepreneur Inc., and the profound impact he has had on the entrepreneurial world. Through a multitude of interviews, speaking engagements, and a ground-breaking book, Robert's influence has transcended borders and touched the lives of countless individuals seeking inspiration, guidance, and resilience.

Magazines from around the world clamoured to interview Robert, eager to uncover the secrets behind his extraordinary success. His insights, honed through years of experience and a relentless pursuit of knowledge, resonated with aspiring entrepreneurs across the globe. With each interview, Robert's message of empowerment, perseverance, and unwavering determination spread like wildfire, igniting the hearts and minds of those who dared to dream.

National TV programs and radio shows sought his wisdom, inviting Robert to share his remarkable journey and the transformative power of Magnetic Entrepreneur Inc. With every appearance, he captivated audiences with his authenticity, charisma, and an unwavering belief in the limitless potential within each individual. As his voice reverberated through the airwaves, hearts were touched, minds were opened, and lives were forever changed.

Robert's unparalleled expertise and magnetic presence led him to share the stage with luminaries in the world of personal development and entrepreneurship. World-class stages became his platform for inspiration, as he stood shoulder-to-shoulder with icons such as Jack Canfield, Les Brown, Bob Proctor, Eric Thomas, Douglas Vermeeren, and Armand Morin. Together, they formed a formidable force, delivering powerful messages that ignited passion, kindled ambition, and propelled individuals toward their greatest aspirations.

But it was Robert's latest endeavour that catapulted him to even greater heights — a book entitled "*Resilience: Based on a True Story.*" This remarkable work, born from the depths of his own life experiences, resonated with readers on a profound level. The book not only graced the iconic billboards of New York Times Square and London Piccadilly Circus, but also caught the attention of Hollywood producers.

Working closely with Robert, a team of talented individuals embarked on the journey to bring "*Resilience*" to the silver screen. The remarkable story of Robert's life, interwoven with themes of triumph, perseverance, and the unwavering spirit of the human soul, had captivated the hearts of readers worldwide. The anticipation grew as the movie adaptation of "*Resilience*" was set to hit theatres in early 2024, promising to inspire audiences with its poignant portrayal of one man's indomitable spirit.

Robert's meteoric rise to prominence was not simply the result of fame and recognition. It was a testament to the unwavering commitment he held for transforming lives and empowering individuals to unlock their fullest potential. Through Magnetic Entrepreneur Inc., he had created a movement — a movement that celebrated resilience, nurtured creativity, and fostered a sense of community that extended far beyond borders.

As we conclude this chapter, we bear witness to the transformative power of Robert J. Moore's work. His interviews, speaking engagements, and the forthcoming movie adaptation of "*Resilience*" serve as a testament to the impact he has had on the lives of countless individuals around the world. Let us now embark on the final segments of this remarkable journey as we explore the legacy that Robert leaves behind and the enduring inspiration his story imparts.

A Legacy of Empowerment

In this final section of Robert J. Moore's extraordinary journey, we delve into the pinnacle of his achievements — the filming of an autobiographical feature that would encapsulate his remarkable life story. This portion explores the enduring legacy of empowerment that Robert leaves behind, inspiring generations to come.

Robert's life had been a tapestry of triumphs, setbacks, and unwavering resilience. The story of his journey, filled with courage, determination, and an unyielding spirit, resonated deeply with individuals from all walks of life. Recognizing the power of his narrative, a team of talented individuals embarked on the monumental task of capturing Robert's life on film.

The process of bringing an autobiography to the screen was no small feat, but with Robert's guidance and the passion of a dedicated film crew, the project took shape. From the early stages of script development to the meticulous casting of actors who would bring his story to life, every detail was carefully curated to ensure authenticity and captivate audiences around the world.

As the cameras rolled, scenes from Robert's childhood unfolded, showcasing the humble beginnings that shaped his indomitable spirit. From his early entrepreneurial ventures to the challenges he faced along the way, the film painted a vivid picture of a man fueled by ambition and an unwavering belief in his own potential.

The autobiographical feature aimed not only to inspire but also to educate. It delved into the strategies, techniques, and mindset shifts that propelled Robert to success, offering a blueprint for aspiring entrepreneurs and individuals seeking to overcome adversity.

Robert J Moore

Robert J. Moore is an accomplished professional featured in Forbes and Disrupt Magazines. As the Founder of Magnetic Entrepreneur Inc., he has built a thriving empire with Magnetic Entrepreneur TV, Business Coaching, and Speaker engagements. Holding two Honorary Doctorate Degrees, Robert is a Guinness World Record holder. Co-authoring books with renowned figures like Kyle Wilson, Todd Stottlemyre, Serena Brown Travis, Armand Morin, Reggie Rusk, and Dr. Joe Vitale.

Robert J. Moore's exceptional accomplishments and dedication to empowering others have solidified his position as an influential leader in the business world.

Social media/contact info

LinkedIn - www.linkedin.com/in/magneticentrepreneur

YouTube
- https://www.youtube.com/c/MagneticEntrepreneurInc

Facebook

Robert J Moore-Magnetic Entrepreneur

Website: https://magnetic-entrepreneur.com/

Upcoming movie: *Resilience Based on a True Story of Robert J. Moore's life*

Upcoming Documentary Film: *Reinventing Freedom: True Documentary of Robert J Moore*

THE POWER OF VIDEO ADVERTISING

Lefteris Koutinas

The word 'advertising' can mean different things to different people because of the endless amount of options that are given to us at the time of writing this chapter. Before I get into the importance of advertising with video specifically, we need to go back a few decades and understand how I got here. I didn't get the name 'Sales Video Jedi' for sitting on my butt doing nothing.

The year is 1952. With each passing day, more and more European immigrants are making their way to Canada, my grandfather being one of them. He probably didn't have a clue as to what he wanted to do when he arrived. But he did know that he needed to pave a path toward a brighter and better future.

I can picture my young, confident grandfather right now, pacing back and forth in what I assume was a tiny one-bedroom apartment asking himself why he came here. What was his purpose (because at the end of the day, it's all about your WHY, am I right?) He didn't come here to work in retail as a stock boy, as a dishwasher in a restaurant, or even as a ticket collector at a movie theatre (although he ended up owning a movie theatre at one point).

He wanted to move people. He wanted to make a change for his community by giving them a voice they could turn to whenever they felt happy, excited, sad, or even alone. So, what was the first thing he set out to do? Do you know? Okay, fine … I'll tell you. He needed to build trust with his community. I remember him telling me this one line when I was 16 years old, which has stuck with me till this day, and that was, *"Get people to fall in love with you, and you'll never be out of business."*

Growing up in a house of media buyers and advertisers helped me build a skill from the 'terrible twos' that I never thought I would use until this day. Grabbing and holding attention, sometimes it was at all costs. Then again, you can't be the loudest person in a noisy market if you aren't willing to ruffle a few feathers. And that's what my grandfather had to do in order to stand out from the competition.

Speaking of "at all costs," we are talking about a guy who can easily shmooze his way into a crowd. He even bought a round or two of drinks for an entire bar once, just because it was entirely filled with his demographic. Now, I don't recommend walking into a bar today and doing that (especially with these inflation rates), but that just goes to show you a glimpse of what it took to literally crush any competition he thought he may have had. When his competitors were playing it safe, he was going all in.

Video is no different. We can be whoever we want to be on video. It's your brand, message, and your time to be unapologetically awesome. Hold yourself to a higher standard. Don't just be another joker giving you three reasons why you shouldn't be doing this or that. I'm sure you can be more exciting than watching paint dry.

The world is full of creators taking mediocre copycat ideas and putting their twist on them. Does it work? Absolutely. Long term? Absolutely not!

My grandfather wouldn't even step out of the house if he wasn't wearing his best suit. He even shaved every single morning without ever skipping a beat (god forbid someone saw him with a bit of scruff). He held himself to a higher standard which also had his listeners and fans hold him to that same standard.

He was moving people every day and I knew it was my turn to do the same. And I did just that. Literally.

You would think that I wanted to follow in my grandfather's footsteps growing up with such a powerful figure, but the truth is, I needed to forge my own path. I remember playing during recess with my friends, and I overheard a conversation about this software called Napster. What an odd name for a computer program, I thought. But as my classmate was going on and on about how he was downloading free music by the dozens, it totally piqued my interest like a deer caught in headlights.

Later that night, I ran to my computer, downloaded the software, and started pirating all my favourite music. It was troublesome to get really clean, crisp CD-quality files which was a huge bummer. I didn't want to spend countless hours trying to search for good quality music either. So I took it up a notch to what you could consider being the dark web of Napster, and at that moment, house music was born.

The perfectly positioned kicks, claps, snares, hi-hats, synths, and basslines shot a rush of dopamine through my body like I'd never felt before. I was only 12 at the time. House music, to me, was just as exciting as the invention of sliced bread. I wanted to do anything and everything I could with this newfound genre of music. By 14 years old, my parents had bought me my first set of turntables, and by 16, I was playing in front of a crowd of 2000 people. I had no idea what I was doing, but I knew what I wanted to play.

I wanted to share my newfound love with as many people as possible. That is the energy you need to bring to your advertising. You need to be excited to plaster your brand everywhere. Picture yourself as the DJ. Your ad (or playlist) is there to evoke emotion and get the crowd (your prospects) to take action. I wasn't a copywriter growing up. I wasn't even an advertiser. I took a few words with me from the wisest person I know and simply ran with it.

It wasn't until I was 21 years old when I found my true voice … or, in this instance, I should say sound. Yes, I had to find my sound. No, not all house music sounds the same. The year was 2009, and I had just taken my first trip to Miami, Florida. Picture ocean drive, a hot summer evening, lights shining as far as the eye could see, drinks flowing, music blaring, and me at the bar just observing.

It was at that moment that I learned what true human psychology was all about. Up until this moment, I was only playing music to play music. That night I witnessed how the women were moving and how the men would just follow like puppy dogs. I also found who my target audience was. Lucky me. Two life lessons in one night. I brought this new information back home with me, and boy, did it ever work. I didn't have words. I had music. That's like trying to sell your audience your product or service, but they're all deaf, so you can't use words. I was slowly becoming unstoppable. And I was taking all my new psychology tactics globally. As more and more years went by, I noticed that there was a slight shift in my audience. They weren't just coming to see me for the music anymore. Their attention shifted toward the performance. They were more interested in how I moved rather than how they moved.

If you think about it, getting in front of a camera, turning on the lights, and pushing the record button is really no different. You're performing. It's the Super Bowl halftime show, and you're the main attraction. My grandfather didn't attract attention and build an entire community from the ground up because of what he said but how he said it. Just like I didn't move dance floors because of what I was playing but how I was playing it, and just like with your video marketing, you see people caught up in what to say, but they forget the "how" is the sizzle to the steak, the whipped cream on the apple pie, and those few additional zero's in your bank account.

As we dive into the depths of video advertising, it's vital to understand that it's not only what you present but how you present it that captivates your audience. Advertising with video is a potent tool. It can transmit a brand's personality, tone, and message in a way that no other medium can, much like music can evoke emotions and make people feel.

Video advertising has the potential to tell a brand's story in a dynamic, visually stimulating way that hits home with the audience. However, to do this effectively, you must understand the art of storytelling. It's not just about flaunting your product or service, but it's also about creating a narrative that your audience can connect with, much like how a DJ curates a set that moves people, inciting them to dance and enjoy the night away.

Consider your brand as the DJ of your audience's lives. As you spin the metaphorical records, you're playing a role in shaping their emotions, perceptions, and actions. Much like a compelling house track, a captivating video advertisement has the potential to transport your audience to an entirely different plane of existence.

For example, if you're advertising a new car, it's not just about the car's features. It's about the thrill of the drive, the prestige that comes with owning the car, or the security it provides for a family. These themes resonate more profoundly with the audience than merely listing technical specifications. Make them feel the wind in their hair as the car zooms down a highway or the peace of mind of seeing their children safely strapped in the back seat. You're selling an experience, an emotion - not just a car.

Being genuine is critical. The audience today can smell inauthenticity a mile away. If you aren't genuine, they'll know it, and you'll lose their trust. This is why you need to create advertisements that are real, that resonate with your audience and are in line with your brand's ethos.

As my grandfather always said, "Get people to fall in love with you, and you'll never be out of business". To do that, you need to go the extra mile. You must create advertisements that leave a lasting impact, that move people, that stir emotions, and ultimately, that drive action.

Much like my journey from a young, house music-loving teenager to a successful DJ, the journey to creating effective video advertising is about trial and error, authenticity, and connecting with your audience. The skills I picked up while creating and playing music are directly applicable to creating and executing a compelling video marketing strategy.

Creating advertisements that strike the right chord with your audience is no easy task. But with the right ingredients - authenticity, understanding of the audience, and a compelling narrative - you can create a masterpiece that will have your audience hooked and coming back for more.

So, channel your inner DJ. Visualize your brand taking center stage, getting the audience dancing to your tunes, capturing their attention and not letting go. The floor is yours, and it's your turn to play.

Your ad is not just a video; it is a performance, a production, and a show that people will remember. Advertising with video is the future, and the future is now. Harness its power, move your audience, and make them fall in love with your brand. After all, as my grandfather said, *"That's the secret to never being out of business."*

Lefteris Koutinas

Lefty's journey in the world of video marketing began by serving as the creative genius behind both 6 and 7-figure coaches, lending his talents to a host of digital campaigns that left a lasting impact on the audience and boosted conversion rates.

He's the video Jedi who's even had his work light up digital billboards, a testament to his boundary-pushing creativity. What sets Lefty apart is his unique brand voice – a punchy mix of snark, sarcasm, self-deprecating humour, and an edgy bite that leaves no room for vanilla.

This unconventional approach is intertwined with real-world events and relatable truths, making his content as engaging as it is emorable. From Video Sales Letters and Story Brand Videos to Commercials and Films, Lefty doesn't believe in one-size-fits-all solutions.

His work is as unique as his clients, with a deep understanding that great content can't simply be rinsed and repeated. Lefty's mission is simple but ambitious: to help businesses unleash their potential through the power of video marketing.

He's already changed the game for many, and he's just getting started. Love him or hate him, you can't ignore Lefty – he's the unconventional maestro who's redefining the landscape of video marketing.

Contact Lefteris (Lefty) Koutinas:

416.824.7540
Book a Call: Website: createwithlefteris.com
Follow: Instagram: instagram.com/createwithlefty

Subscribe: Youtube Channel: youtube.com/@createwithlefty

FROM SILENT TO SUCCESSFUL: THE JOURNEY OF A FORMER INTROVERT AND PASTOR TO BECOMING A 7-FIGURE SALES NINJA

Jay Lee

Matchless Work Ethic

Growing up in a Korean Canadian immigrant family taught me the value of hard work and determination. My parents, despite their impressive educational background, had to start from scratch in a new country, Canada and had no friends and didn't know English.

They had to go back to school and take their degrees over again in a language they didn't understand. My two older brothers and I were latchkey kids, which basically meant we were given a house key and were home alone other than our grandmother, who didn't know any English.

As latchkey kids, my brothers and I learned to fend for ourselves at a young age. Family time and vacations were mere fantasies, and financial struggles were a constant companion. Please do not misunderstand me, my parents sacrificed everything they had to give us a better life, and eventually, they did twenty-plus years later.

My parents worked multiple jobs; namely, my mom worked twelve-hour graveyard shifts at the hospital in downtown Toronto, and instead of going home to sleep, she went straight to my dad's sandwich shop, where she worked another twelve hours. She didn't sleep much for at least five years.

Nothing came on a silver platter, as you can imagine. If we achieved a 92% grade, they would ask where the other 8% went. If we weren't number one, the question was, why not? We were constantly compared to others who were doctors, dentists, and lawyers.

I remember practising the piano for three hours daily for years to complete my Royal Conservatory of Piano at the highest level, which, thanks to my parents, I achieved. I want to thank my parents for pushing me hard when I didn't feel like it and when I wanted to quit, which seemed like a daily thought. It reminded me of the quote by David Goggins, former navy seal,

"Everybody comes to a point in their life when they want to quit. But it's what you do at that moment that determines who you are."

It was during these challenging times that I made a solemn promise to myself: I would change the course of my family's future. Not only did I want to break the cycle of generational poverty, but I also dreamed of creating a new future of abundance and giving.

Triumph and Humiliation

Despite my struggle to find my voice, I excelled academically, musically, and athletically. I even skipped two grades and earned a place at one of Canada's top universities. However, deep-rooted insecurities still lingered within me. In grade 4, my fear of rejection reached its peak when my teacher would not allow me to go to the washroom.

I asked three times, and she yelled back at me, telling me to wait until recess. I wasn't able to hold it in anymore, so I walked to the back of the classroom behind the metal revolving book rack in shame as I peed my pants. I felt so defeated. I was so ashamed. The humiliation was crushing, but it served as a catalyst for change. I grew increasingly dissatisfied with staying silent and not using my voice. It was time for a change, but it wouldn't happen overnight.

A Voice Muted

In the early years of my life, I found myself unable to speak up for fear of judgment and rejection. In middle school, my voice failed me when my guidance teacher asked me a simple question. All the students, including the teacher, laughed at me. I vividly recall a moment when my parents left me alone in the car to buy cold-cut meats for the delicatessen to explain to the police not to issue a parking ticket and that my parents were coming back shortly.

Paralyzed by fear, I cowered in the backseat in a fetal position, unable to speak up, let alone make my presence known. This silence haunted me, becoming a symbol of my insecurities.

Breaking Free

As high school approached, I faced new challenges that tested my courage. I was the quiet, shy guy who people missed and was overlooked when being chosen for group projects and team sports.

Little did they know that I was the guy who skipped two grades, was a straight-A student and excelled at piano, mathematics, and sports. I would practise my trade for hours in silence, all alone. Shooting, dribbling, practising scales, and working ten times harder than the average student.

I was the underdog. Nobody knew who I was and what I was capable of doing. I continued to be silent in hopes that people would notice or elevate me to the place I belonged, but that never happened.

In fact, there was a girl I had a crush on in my last year of high school, but my insecurities and lack of confidence held me back from asking her to the prom. The weight of missed opportunities began to weigh heavily on me. I yearned for the strength to break free from my self-imposed limitations. I said enough is enough.

My turning point came when I finally mustered enough courage to confront my fear of rejection. This was my last chance. I saw my high school crush in the library on the last day before the prom. In the most awkward way possible, I caught her leaving, and I stood and blocked the exit.

I realize now how creepy and weird that was. My two friends, both computer geeks (yes, I hung around this crowd), watched from behind the book shelves giggling at my desperate attempt to win her heart. She looked shocked, almost as if she never heard me talk, which was probably the case.

When she asked me how I could help her, I mumbled and squirmed and somehow found the words to ask her out to the prom. Her response seemed like it took an eternity. You could hear a pin drop, and time stopped. Her response was, "Oh, that's so sweet, Jay. I wish you had asked me earlier. Someone already asked me to the prom."

I nearly dropped dead in facing rejection, but also felt relief that I overcame my fear of finding my voice and breaking free. Again, I became smaller in the face of failure.

A Higher Calling

I flunked out of one of the top Canadian universities, and I can remember the day I shared the bad news with my parents. My mom cried out in pain and shame, and I felt so defeated that I failed my parents. After much reflection, focusing on developing my character and applying myself that summer after getting kicked out, I wrote a heartfelt letter to the dean of science and basically begged for a second chance.

Miraculously by the grace of God, which is what it had to be, I got accepted again, and I never looked back. I studied my butt off and worked as if my life depended on it, which in some ways, it did. This is when my future wife, Vivian, entered the scene. It was a setup from God. If she had met me six months earlier, she would have laughed at the clown that I was. But I was a completely different person.

I had faced too much failure and defeat in my life, and I decided to fall forward, lick my wounds, and fight back. Not only did I find my true identity, but I also found my voice and asked Vivian out. She said yes. And we eventually got married.

After graduating from university, I felt a calling to serve others and make a positive impact on their lives. I became a pastor, dedicating myself to helping those in need. For 15 years, I poured my heart and soul into my work, but financial struggles eventually forced me to reconsider my path. With a salary of only $1,000 per month, I could no longer support my wife and three young kids.

Pivoting and Discovering a Hidden Talent

With the weight of responsibility pressing on my shoulders, I embarked on a journey of self-discovery. Recognizing the need to provide for my loved ones, I decided to pivot. Drawing on my past experiences and newfound determination, I delved into the world of sales. To my surprise, I discovered a hidden talent — a knack for closing high-ticket sales.

The Birth of a Vision

Armed with my newfound skill and an unwavering determination to transform lives, I established a Sales Coaching business. My vision was to empower online entrepreneurs with the ability to sell their high-ticket offers effectively, enabling them to achieve their dreams of financial freedom, quality family time, and the opportunity to impact others positively.

Overcoming Mindset Barriers

With dedication and perseverance, I began selling $100,000+ per month in revenue on a part-time basis while juggling a full-time job, three young children, and a brand-new puppy.

This success shattered my poverty mindset and ignited an even greater passion within me. I realized that I had the potential to create a business that could change lives on a massive scale.

Embracing the Journey

My transformative story motivated me to take a leap of faith. Leaving behind my past, I fully committed to my Sales Coaching business. I knew that by pursuing my mission, I could help countless entrepreneurs overcome their fears, sell like crazy without sounding 'salesy,' and achieve the freedom they had always yearned for.

Empowering Others

Today, I stand as a testament to the power of perseverance and the potential for personal transformation. Through my coaching, I empower individuals to find their voice, overcome their limitations, and build businesses that exceed their wildest dreams.

The impact I make reaches far beyond financial success — it extends to the freedom to spend quality time with loved ones, travel the world, and make a meaningful difference in the lives of others.

Epilogue: A Global Movement

My journey from an introverted and silenced individual to a successful entrepreneur has inspired a global movement. The GLASS Selling Framework, based on my own experiences and expertise, has revolutionized the way coaches and online entrepreneurs sell their products and services.

By embracing authenticity and leveraging powerful sales techniques, countless individuals have found the courage to speak up, win in life, and accomplish their dreams.

In conclusion, my underdog story resonates with anyone who has ever felt trapped by their own insecurities. Through my struggles and triumphs, I have discovered the transformative power of embracing one's true potential.

By utilizing the GLASS Selling Framework, I have not only achieved financial success but also unlocked the ability to impact lives on a grand scale. No longer silenced, I stand tall as a beacon of hope and inspiration for all those who dare to dream and strive for greatness. My hope and prayer is that you sell more to give more. Feel free to join my free Facebook Group community to learn more at

www.facebook.com/groups/salesninjacommunity

Jay Lee

Jay Lee is a world-class high ticket closer and sales coach. He's also known as the Sales Ninja and helps high ticket coaches and entrepreneurs sell like crazy without sounding 'salesy,' sleazy or making prospects sleepy with boring offers using the proven GLASS Selling Method. This GLASS Method has generated $25M+ in client revenue and continues to empower his clients to sell more to give more.

His G.L.A.S.S. Selling Method is a 5-Step Framework That Closed $1M+ in 12 Weeks with close rates as high as 81% and cash collection rates as high as 96% for consecutive months. He was interviewed by Eli Wilde's podcast, amongst many others and helped a recent client scale from $0-$2.5M in 24 months.

He is on a mission to help 1,000 coaches and online entrepreneurs sell more to give more.

EMBRACING CHALLENGES, CONQUERING DREAMS: A JOURNEY OF RESILIENCE AND SUCCESS

Krystle Aquino-Idago

A Humble Beginning

Hello, I am Krystle. At the age of 40, I am a proud wife and mother of three beautiful children, Mathieu, Zoe and Noah, aged 14, 12, and 10.

My life has been an incredible rollercoaster ride, full of twists and turns, challenges, and triumphs. Today, as I reflect on my journey, I am grateful for every obstacle I encountered, as they moulded me into the strong, resilient woman I am today.

The Path of Endless Opportunities

Throughout my life, I embraced various roles and professions, each serving as stepping stones toward personal growth and self-discovery. From my humble beginnings as a waitress at Pizza Hut to working as a receptionist in a shoe factory and later as a receptionist in a prestigious 5-star hotel in Brussels, Belgium, I learned the importance of dedication, perseverance, and service.

As fate would have it, I found myself employed by an American multinational during the tumultuous financial crisis of 2008. Although the company's downsizing resulted in my unfortunate dismissal, it ignited a spark within me — a spark that fueled my desire to create something extraordinary.

The Birth of Entrepreneurial Spirit

In collaboration with my loving husband, we embarked on an entrepreneurial journey. Together, we established a cleaning agency

~ 25 ~

for households, which soon became the cornerstone of our business empire. We were determined to build a life where we could be present for our children, never separated from them, and never miss any of their milestones.

Despite the challenges we faced, we never lost sight of our goals. Our business thrived, and after celebrating 11 successful years with our dedicated employees, we realized that our little venture had transformed into an enterprise that served over a thousand clients with a workforce of 150 employees. Dreams, when nurtured with unwavering dedication, can indeed bear magnificent fruits.

Conquering the Unforeseen Battle

Just as our business began to flourish, life threw an unexpected curveball at me. After giving birth to my third child, I was diagnosed with thyroid cancer — a diagnosis that shook my world to its core. Yet, I refused to let this illness define me. With unwavering determination and the support of my loved ones, I embarked on a journey of healing.

As I battled this dreadful "C", I discovered the true power of resilience. Through the darkest moments, I sought GOD's refuge, our merciful creator. I acknowledged HIS gift of the belief that I was destined for greater things. With each passing day, I fought my way back to health, emerging as a survivor — a testament to the indomitable human spirit.

The Power of Faith and Divine Timing

My journey would not be complete without acknowledging the impact of faith in my life. Raised by my grandparents after my parents left to work overseas, I often yearned for their presence and longed for a reunion. At the tender age of 14, my 'wish-upon-a-star' was granted, and I was finally reunited with my beloved parents.

Throughout my experiences, I have come to realize that we are all made in God's image and likeness, equipped with the strength and resources needed to overcome any obstacle. As Joyce Meyer once said, *"You may be in a tough time, but you have to say, 'I'm equipped, empowered, and anointed to get through this."* With faith as my guiding light, I conquered adversity and turned my dreams into reality.

Navigating the Storms: A Resilient Mindset

In the face of the ongoing pandemic, our business faced unprecedented challenges.

I am constantly reminded of the wisdom of James Allen, who said, *"The outer conditions of a person's life will always be found to reflect their inner beliefs."* Armed with an unwavering belief in our purpose and the power of adaptability, we weathered the storm.

We transformed our business model, adapted to innovations, and found new ways to connect with our clients and employees. Through it all, we stayed committed to providing exceptional service, and our annual recurring income reached astounding euros.

This success during difficult times serves as a testament to the fact that we truly have all the resources we need within us to overcome any challenge.

The Call to Action: Now is the Time

Dear readers, as you immerse yourself in my journey, I invite you to reflect upon your own dreams and aspirations. As Napoleon Hill wisely said, *"Whatever the mind can conceive and believe, it can achieve."* Now is the time to act, for there is no better moment than the present to pursue your dreams.

Embrace the teachings of John Maxwell, Bob Proctor, Earl Nightingale, Wallace Wattles, Angela Duckworth, Jose Silva, and Victor Frankl. Draw inspiration from their wisdom, for they have paved the way for countless individuals to overcome adversity and achieve greatness. Remember, you are capable of creating your own success story.

The Power of Unity and Gratitude

As I conclude my story, I am filled with immense gratitude — for the challenges, the triumphs, the setbacks, and the victories. They have fashioned me into this optimist that defies obstacles. It taught me invaluable lessons along the way. I am eternally grateful for the unwavering support of my husband, my beautiful children, my dear and loving Mom and Dad and the incredible team that stood by us through thick and thin.

Together, we have proven that dreams are not merely figments of imagination but powerful catalysts for transformation. With a resilient mindset, unwavering faith, and an unyielding determination, we can conquer any obstacle and achieve the extraordinary.

So, dear reader, I implore you — embrace your dreams, for they are the roadmap to your destiny. Take a leap of faith, trust in your abilities, and remember that you are equipped with everything you need to turn your dreams into reality. Now is the time to act, for the world eagerly awaits your unique brilliance.

Unleashing the Power Within

Within each of us lies a reservoir of untapped potential waiting to be unleashed. As we navigate the journey of life, it is essential to harness our inner strength and tap into the limitless power that resides within us. The teachings of great minds like Bob Proctor, Les Brown, and Andrew Carnegie remind us that we are capable of achieving greatness if we dare to believe in ourselves.

In today's fast-paced and ever-changing world, it is easy to succumb to self-doubt and fear. Nevertheless, I encourage you to silence that inner voice of doubt and replace it with a resounding belief in your abilities. I am a hopeless optimist.

Les Brown said,

"You have greatness within you. Believe it, think about it, dream about it, and BECOME it."

Take a moment to reflect on your unique strengths, talents, and passions.

What sets your soul on fire? What dreams have you tucked away in the depths of your heart? Now is the time to bring them to the surface, for within them lies the blueprint for your ultimate success.

The Power of Mindset and Persistence

As we embark on our individual journeys, it is crucial to cultivate a growth mindset — one that sees challenges as opportunities for growth and views setbacks as temporary "detours" rather than permanent roadblocks.

The wisdom of Earl Nightingale reminds us,

"Success is the progressive realization of a worthy ideal."

Adopting a growth mindset allows us to persevere in the face of adversity, for we understand that failure is not a reflection of our worth but an integral part of the learning process. As we encounter obstacles along the way, let us remember the words of Napoleon Hill, who said,

"Every adversity, every failure, every heartache carries with it the seed of an equal or greater benefit."

Persistence, coupled with a growth mindset, can propel us toward our goals and dreams. Take heart in the teachings of Andrew Carnegie, who believed that PERSISTENCE is the key to success.

Trust in your ability to overcome any obstacle and persevere even when the path seems arduous.

Be constantly reminded that SUCCESS often lies just beyond the point where most people give up.

Cultivating the Habits of Success

Success is not a result of chance or luck; it is born from the consistent cultivation of positive habits. Take a page from the book of Wallace Wattles, who emphasized the power of daily actions in shaping our reality. By consciously choosing habits that align with our goals, we lay the foundation for lasting success.

One such habit is that of continuous learning.

Commit yourself to lifelong learning and personal development. Dive into books, attend seminars, and seek out mentors who can guide you on your journey. Angela Duckworth quotes,

"Grit is living life like it's a marathon, not a sprint."

Embrace the mindset of constant growth and improvement.

Moreover, practice GRATITUDE daily. Express appreciation for the blessings in your life, no matter how small. Gratitude shifts our focus from scarcity to abundance and opens the door to new opportunities. As Joyce Meyer wisely stated,

"Gratitude is one of the sweet shortcuts to finding peace of mind and happiness inside."

Embracing Challenges as Catalysts for Growth

Throughout my journey, I have encountered numerous challenges, each presenting an opportunity for growth and self-discovery.

Taking on challenges as catalysts for growth requires a shift in perspective. Rather than viewing them as roadblocks, see them as stepping stones toward your desired destination.

Embrace the teachings of Jose Silva, who believed that every problem contains the seed of its own solution. Approach challenges with a problem-solving mindset, knowing that within them lies the key to your personal and professional growth. Remember, the greatest lessons are often learned in the face of adversity.

Living a Life of Purpose and Impact

As we strive for success, it is crucial to align our actions with a greater purpose. James Allen profoundly stated,

"Dream lofty dreams, and as you dream, so shall you become."

Take the time to discover your purpose, your "why." What impact do you wish to make in the world? How do you want to be remembered?

When our actions are fueled by a sense of purpose, they transcend mere personal gain. We become agents of change, inspiring others to fulfil their dreams and live up to their maximum potential. As Victor Frankl beautifully articulated,

"What is to give light must endure the burning."

Embrace the journey, knowing that your purpose is worth every sacrifice and effort.

Now is the Time for Action

Dear reader, as you reach the end of my story, I urge you to take action now.

The present moment is all we have, and there is no better time to chase your dreams and transform your life.

As Bob Proctor famously said,

"Set a goal to achieve something that is so big, so exhilarating that it excites you and scares you at the same time."

Funny, true and really scary!

But no other course to take but that way, facing and trudging the steps towards the PUZZLE ahead.

You possess within you the power to create the life you desire. You are equipped with the necessary resources and talents to turn your dreams into reality. Believe in yourself, trust in your abilities, and take that first step toward your dreams.

Remember, the world needs your unique brilliance and the impact you are destined to make. Embrace the teachings of John Maxwell, Bob Proctor, Earl Nightingale, Andrew Carnegie, Les Brown, Napoleon Hill, Wallace Wattles, Angela Duckworth, Joyce Meyer, Jose Silva, James Allen, and Victor Frankl. Draw inspiration from their wisdom and let their words guide you on your path to success.

Now, dear reader, it is time to unleash your greatness and embark on your own extraordinary journey. Embrace the power within you and live a life that truly reflects your dreams, purpose, and potential.

The time is now.

Seize it with unwavering determination, and let your success story unfold.

Lastly, I want to leave this message with you. Always remember, where you are now doesn't matter. Where you are going does. Remember to get "Krystle-Clear" wherever you go.

Krystle Aquino-Idago

Krystle Aquino-Idago is an embodiment of the power of dreams and the courage to pursue them. Born in the Philippines and now a dual citizen of Belgium and the Philippines, Krystle is a 40-year-old entrepreneur, life coach, and mindset coach.

Her journey began with humble beginnings, working as a waitress and a receptionist in various industries. However, she faced a significant setback during the 2008 financial crisis when she was let go from her job at an American multinational corporation. It was during this challenging period that Krystle's unwavering determination and resilience emerged.

Not only did she triumph over thyroid cancer, celebrating nine years of being cancer-free, but she also refused to let circumstances define her. Krystle and her husband Jon, fueled by their shared vision, started their entrepreneurial journey, establishing eight successful businesses. Their main venture, a thriving cleaning agency for households, has flourished, boasting 150 employees and serving countless clients. Despite the hardships of the pandemic, their annual recurring income now reaches an impressive seven figures.

Krystle's story is a testament to the incredible possibilities that await those who dare to dream and take action. She and her husband made a conscious choice to build a life where they would never miss their children's milestones. Their entrepreneurial ventures provided the means to shape their own destiny and create a future filled with freedom, fulfillment, and family togetherness.

Now, as a passionate life coach and mindset coach, Krystle inspires others to step out of their comfort zones and pursue their own dreams. Through her guidance and personal experiences, she encourages individuals to tap into their true potential, overcome obstacles, and create a life they are genuinely passionate about.

Krystle Aquino-Idago's journey serves as a powerful reminder that dreams are within reach, no matter the circumstances. Her story ignites a spark within others, urging them to take bold steps towards their aspirations. With unwavering determination, resilience, and the belief that anything is possible, Krystle's mission is to empower individuals to act on their dreams and create a life filled with purpose, joy, and limitless possibilities.

THE GRACE TO LEAD WITH A HEALTHY SOUL

Yvette C. Owens

How many times have you allowed a thought to become an outburst or an action, and looking back at it, you wondered, "Where in the world did that come from?" We are not so concerned when there is little to no impact on anyone other than ourselves. What do we do when a behaviour trait goes unchecked and negatively impacts our performance or, worse, how we lead people?

The stuff - let's call it what it really is, the junk in our souls can get us into a lot of trouble. We justify our behaviour too often by qualifying it as 'the nature of doing business' or 'that is simply how the game is played.' I am calling for a revamping of the game's rules. I am challenging every leader to complete a deep inspection and cleansing of how you lead others. Mustard up the courage to vow to lead with grace – the grace you would like to receive from others.

Grace is absolutely required when evaluating your soul. Without applying grace to our past, we tend to respond in one of the following ways:

Fight the messenger.

Deny what is evident.

Run from what we find.

Justify poor behaviour.

Act guilt-ridden.

Blame others.

Cover it up.

Try to fix it quickly.

Every one of the above responses is a temporary remedy because we don't take the time to consider the root cause and source of what we are expressing. I would venture in most cases, we are embarrassed to some degree and would do anything to undo the poorly managed moment. Yet, some of us keep plowing down the road expecting that it will all turn out alright and no one will remember. People always remember how you leave them feeling, especially when it is unexpected. The unexpected response happens when you leave them feeling good or bad. Have you had someone show you great appreciation for a very small gesture? Your act of kindness was huge to that individual. I sometimes think that small gestures are so powerful now because society, at large, has become so harsh and hard. Shout, "Opportunity!" We have the opportunity to shine brightly in a world where vast ends of the spectrum are working in tandem, making life more complex.

Let's examine some scenarios to get a perspective of the polarizing circumstances we are facing, especially in the business community. Organization one experiences difficulty hiring new leaders and staff, while organization two has new hires flocking to their openings. Some employees feel trapped in their current position, while many employees recognize that the sky is the limit as they apply to other organizations for their ideal position. I recently shared an article that some employees resorted to creating and building a side business while working for their employer. Employee engagement surveys are not being responded to effectively. The span of responsibility for leaders is getting broader and deeper in the organization with little reward,s if any. The organizations that check in with their employee resource groups are finding that the efforts to give the employees voices have results that are too little, too late. Human Resource specialists are fighting for the right formulas to maintain diversity, equity and inclusion at its purest definition without offending any people group.

We all need a little more grace!

Grace

Dean James Ryan defines grace during his address to the Harvard Graduate School of Education 2017 diploma and certificate recipients as follows:

"To lead with grace, to me, means to lead with gratitude and with courage. It means to lead with forgiveness and to lead in the service of others. It means to lead with authenticity and with a combination of confidence and humility." 1

A Healthy Soul

"The soul corresponds to the heart-brain connection. A healthy soul helps you experience positive emotions such as joy and gratitude, emotional resilience, kindness and compassion toward others, and a sense of purpose and being connected to something greater than yourself." 2

My Grace Walk

The truth is that I am learning every day to lead with more grace all because of what I have suffered in the workplace as a leader. My leadership style started as intimidating out of fear of failure. I was a hard taskmaster requiring perfection from myself and those on my teams. I was in a spiritual setting and challenged by a spiritual leader as to why I half-heartedly joked about knowing that I could be intimidating to others. Admittedly. I wore a badge of honour to some degree. Writing this now and after a period during my career of reporting to harsh, sabotaging leaders, I am experiencing deep regret. This would be a moment of "Where did that come from?" I know exactly where it came from. We emulate what we learn. However, being on the opposite side of such harassment and abuse, I would never again lead in that manner.

Clearly, there were holes in my soul at that time from imposter syndrome and trying to survive in a culture where I was not welcome as my authentic self. I remember sharing lunch with a group of colleagues, and during the conversation, I blurted out, "I want my joy back." My soul cried out for refreshing and reviving. I determined that I would do the work to get my joy and peace back. I vowed never to let anyone steal my joy and peace ever again. I don't care what position or title a person holds; I guard my soul, mind and heart against mistreatment and control by another person. It is from a place of healing in my soul that grace shows in my leadership style. No one should ever have to suffer due to another person's sick soul. Leaders need frequent check-ups in this area to optimize the grace released in their daily transactions and transformations of themselves and their teams. It is a privilege to lead from the heart to influence others to do the same. The transformation in individuals, the outcomes produced, and the relationships developed are more than worth the effort and vigilance it takes to grow in grace.

During the hardest and lowest point of my career, I needed much grace. I was under attack by a leadership team that entered the organization with their entire entourage. The group of leaders sought to discredit those of us who had a history with the organization. I felt as though I was in a fight for my life. I recount the experience in my book, *"Conquering Corporate Enemies: Mind. Personalities. Situations"*. Once I came to grips with the fact that I needed help to sort out what was happening and to forgive myself for not having a stronger self-identity, one that could not be shaken by anyone, I found grace, allyship and advocates in a friend, former leader and former client. All three were gracious enough to walk me through the process of learning that my reputation in the organization was still solid and intact despite the rumours and negativity around me. These individuals were helpful and not accusatory, helping me to focus on the next steps I could take, and they provided tangible assistance in getting me to a healthier place.

In hindsight, it was good that I experienced that hardship to become the leader I am today. I gained the courage to reflect constantly on my performance to ensure that I am operating in grace. Even when I make a mistake, I learn from the mistake, apologize to those impacted by my actions and make the necessary adjustments to correct the error. Since I learned to give myself grace, I am able to give others grace. Grace doesn't cause you to run a weak organization. The contrary is true. Grace creates an organization of excellence where we take the time to celebrate success and determine how we can together improve our experience.

I must admit that it has taken me some time to really forgive those who tried to destroy me during a time when I was building my career and continuing to provide for my daughter as a divorced mom. Yes, it is true that unforgiveness keeps the person who refuses to forgive trapped in bondage. I got tired of them occupying space in my head and heart. I wanted my soul to be whole.

I now have the honour of coaching C-Level leaders to lead with soul, healthy souls. Organizations must be thriving cultures for all. I help leaders who are overwhelmed with implementing their strategies and who feel alone and distant from their team to reconnect with their superpower and regain their voice to strengthen, equip and position their teams for greater success with my *5 step DestinySpeak Outloud* coaching program using the V.I.C.T.O.R. framework.

Leading with grace and cultivating a healthy soul is not an easy task. Still, it is a transformative journey that can revolutionize your leadership style and your organization's culture. By prioritizing authenticity, forgiveness, gratitude, and compassion, you can create an environment where individuals fulfill their purpose while achieving the organization's vision.

1 "Lead With Grace" by Dean James Ryan, Harvard Graduate School of Education

2 "Out-of-Sorts? Strengthening Your Mind, Body, Soul Connection Can Help" by Erin Eatough, PhD

Yvette C. Owens

Yvette C Owens is a world-renowned speaker, international best-selling author, leadership coach, and consultant who teaches C-Level leaders to lead with soul using change leadership principles to increase adoption, retain talent, and build high-performing teams using the proprietary V.I.C.T.O.R. framework. Yvette, aka Changologist, is a board-certified change management professional (A.C.M.P.).

She has 40+ years of sharing her vibrant, resilience, compassion, and influence in teaching *"Dealing With Resistance To Accept And Invest In Change"* during keynote speeches and live and virtual working sessions.

Client Review

"Yvette is very knowledgeable in project management and professional development. On several occasions, Yvette customized training for my team. She took the necessary time to understand my objectives and the needs of my team and over delivered. Yvette is at the top of my list for professional development consulting and project management. I highly recommend Yvette." ~ David Daye, Goodwin University

Books

No Bosses Allowed | | Lead to Serve & Transform (eBook & Online Course)

Conquering Corporate Enemies: Mind. Personalities. Situations (Book & Workbook)

The Creatives: Leadership

Speakers Highlights

Catalent Pharma Solutions

SCORE Western Massachusetts

Hartford Women's Leadership Summit

The Kapptor Connection Conference

TAG Talks (VIP Speaker)

Book Reviews: Conquering Corporate Enemies: Mind. Personalities. Situations.

"You Nailed It! Addressing the issues of workplace discontent and challenges is not an easy topic. However, the author has done a great job of addressing these complicated situations." ~ Lady Diva T

"I wanted to thank you for paving the way for other African Americans/West Indians. Your strength, intelligence, and perseverance have made you a great role model. I know I would not survive walking in your shoes. Thank you, and continue being who you are because you are an inspiration." ~ Lisa Mair

Contact Information

Email: VisionToReality@DestinySpeak.com

LinkedIn: Yvette (Cary) Owens | LinkedIn

Facebook: Yvette C. Owens | Facebook

Instagram: DestinySpeak (@destinyspeak) • Instagram photos and videos

Website: DestinySpeak Leadership & Organization Development Company

Success and Leadership are Inevitable with Self-Worth Alignment and Self-Love.

Marianne Padjan

Success and leadership are inevitable when you learn to align your self-worth with self-love. In this day and age, it is crucial to understand that true leadership comes from within. Before you can lead others, you first need to lead yourself. This chapter delves into how self-love and self-worth can lead you to success and to become a great leader.

Self-Love: The Key to Personal Leadership

Many believe that self-love is the secret to happiness and success. In today's fast-paced world, it is easy to forget to love and take care of oneself. However, it is essential to develop a deep and loving relationship with oneself before anything else.

The reason being when you love yourself, you automatically become more confident, clear, and motivated. It enables you to take on challenges without fear and promotes better physical and emotional health.

Self-Worth: The Key to Professional Leadership

Self-worth refers to the degree of an individual's value and respect for themselves. A person who has high self-worth is confident, assertive, and doesn't compare themselves to others.

Self-worth is essential when it comes to professional leadership. Many times, people may be willing to lead but may not believe they are enough.

It is vital to work on your self-worth and believe in yourself. When you understand your value, you automatically understand what you can bring to the table, and in turn, you inspire others to see their worth.

Alignment: The Key to Consistent Leadership

Self-love and self-worth are essential, but it is vital to align these two concepts. When you align self-love with self-worth, it means that you inherently believe that you are loved and worthy.

Aligning self-love with self-worth creates a balance that leads to consistent leadership. It's like having a GPS guiding you step by step toward your goals.

When you align self-love and self-worth, you become more conscious of your thoughts, emotions, and actions. You make conscious decisions and are more authentic, making it easier for you to lead.

Conclusion:

In summary, self-love and self-worth should be at the forefront of your mind when it comes to success and leadership. This is an inside job!

You must go deep inside of you and address whatever the blockages are that are preventing you from forward movement. This could be from your childhood, a past relationship or a place of employment.

It could also be a person in your family, at work, or school, a partner (personal or business) or YOU! Let yourself out of the self-prison you have created.

When you work on your inner self, you become more poised to lead and inspire others. Therefore, it is vital to take the time to love and value yourself, which will enable you to be a successful and consistent leader.

You are enough, and you can be the leader you were born to be.

THIS, TO ME, IS SUCCESS!

LOVE & LIGHT

Marianne Padjan

Marianne has been helping people with their real estate needs for 10-plus years. She has been a partner with EXP REALTY BROKERAGE for almost two years now. She enjoys helping people find their homes and investment properties.

Marianne also enjoys writing as she is a 5-time International Best-Selling Award-Winning author, CEO of MPowered Voice Publishing, co-Owner at MagneticFM radio, with *REAL ESTATE INS and OUTS BOOK*, RADIO SHOW and TV Podcast show.

As an empowerment coach, she also enjoys facilitating workshops and retreats as well as masterminds.

Contact Marianne at:

Spiritualtouch11@gmail.com

EMPOWERING BUSINESSES AND TRANSFORMING LIVES: THE CADJPRO PAYROLL SOLUTIONS JOURNEY

Garcia Hanson-Francis

Introduction

In this chapter, we will delve into the inspiring story of Garcia and CADJPRO Payroll Solutions, a boutique payroll firm dedicated to providing payroll and accounting services to small businesses across Canada.

With a passion for empowering companies and individuals, Garcia has built CADJPRO Payroll Solutions from the ground up, transforming it into a driving force for upliftment and growth.

In today's competitive business landscape, small businesses often face numerous challenges, including managing complex payroll and accounting processes. However, amidst these challenges, CADJPro Payroll Solutions has emerged as a beacon of hope, offering comprehensive payroll and accounting services tailored specifically for small businesses across Canada.

This uplifting story highlights the incredible impact CADJPro has had on countless companies, illuminating the transformative power of their services. This chapter will explore the various ways in which Garcia and her firm contribute to uplifting businesses and people, leaving a lasting impact on the lives they touch.

The Birth of CADJPro Payroll Solutions

CADJPro Payroll Solutions was founded by Garcia Hanson-Francis, a Payroll Leadership Professional with a vision to simplify the payroll and accounting processes for small businesses. Fueled by her passion for empowering entrepreneurs, Garcia established CADJPro Payroll Solutions, a boutique firm that would provide comprehensive and personalized payroll and accounting services to small businesses across Canada.

Creating Tailored Solutions

One of the key ways in which CADJPRO Payroll Solutions uplifts businesses is by offering customized solutions that address their unique payroll and accounting needs. Garcia understands that every company is different, and a one-size-fits-all approach does not work.

With a keen eye for detail and a commitment to excellence, CADJPRO takes the time to understand each client's requirements, challenges, and goals. By tailoring their services, Garcia ensures that businesses receive accurate, efficient, and personalized solutions, allowing them to focus on their core competencies and drive growth.

Streamlining Payroll Processes

Managing payroll can be a daunting task for small businesses, often consuming valuable time and resources. Garcia recognized this pain point and made it her mission to streamline payroll processes for her clients. CADJPRO Payroll Solutions leverages cutting-edge technology and automation tools to simplify and expedite payroll administration.

By implementing efficient systems and processes, Garcia eliminates the complexities and redundancies associated with payroll management. This empowers businesses to allocate their resources more effectively, enabling them to invest time and energy into activities that drive productivity and profitability.

Ensuring Regulatory Compliance

Navigating the ever-changing landscape of payroll legislation is a challenge for businesses of all sizes. Garcia understands the importance of compliance and the severe consequences that non-compliance can have on businesses. CADJPRO Payroll Solutions stays up-to-date with the latest payroll regulations, ensuring that clients remain compliant with government requirements. By meticulously adhering to legal obligations, Garcia and her team alleviate the burden of payroll compliance for businesses, providing them with peace of mind and allowing them to focus on their core operations.

Enhancing Accuracy and Reliability

Payroll errors can have a significant impact on both businesses and employees. Garcia recognizes the importance of accuracy and reliability in payroll processing and makes it a priority within CADJPRO Payroll Solutions.

Through meticulous attention to detail, rigorous quality checks, and a commitment to precision, Garcia ensures that clients' payroll is handled with utmost accuracy and timeliness. By minimizing errors and discrepancies, CADJPRO empowers businesses to maintain a positive relationship with their employees, fostering trust, loyalty, and productivity.

Confidentiality and Data Security

In an era of increasing cyber threats and data breaches, safeguarding sensitive payroll information is paramount. Garcia understands the critical importance of data security and takes stringent measures to protect client data.

CADJPRO Payroll Solutions implements robust security protocols, encryption methods, and access controls to ensure the confidentiality and integrity of payroll data. By prioritizing data security, Garcia creates a safe and trustworthy environment for businesses to entrust their sensitive information, fostering long-term relationships built on trust and reliability.

Providing Expert Guidance and Support

Garcia and her team at CADJPRO Payroll Solutions bring a wealth of expertise and knowledge to the table. They stay abreast of the latest developments in the payroll and accounting industry, continually upgrading their skills and staying updated with best practices. This expertise enables CADJPRO to provide businesses with valuable guidance and support beyond payroll processing.

Whether it's advising on payroll-related tax implications, offering insights on cost-saving measures, or assisting with financial planning, Garcia and her team go the extra mile to empower their clients with comprehensive support and advice.

Nurturing Client Relationships

At CADJPRO Payroll Solutions, fostering strong and enduring client relationships is a core value. Garcia firmly believes in the power of collaboration and partnership. She cultivates an environment of open communication, active listening, and responsiveness.

By truly understanding the unique challenges and aspirations of each client, Garcia builds long-lasting relationships based on trust, empathy, and mutual growth. Through ongoing support, regular feedback, and proactive problem-solving, CADJPRO becomes a trusted advisor and an integral part of the clients' journey toward success.

Unleashing the Power of Efficiency

Small businesses often struggle with managing payroll and accounting tasks, which can be time-consuming and complex. CADJPro Payroll Solutions stepped in with their expertise, implementing streamlined systems and processes to eliminate unnecessary administrative burdens.

Their team of skilled professionals leveraged state-of-the-art software to automate payroll calculations, tax deductions, and employee recordkeeping, ensuring accuracy and compliance with regulatory requirements.

Striving for Client Success

For CADJPro Payroll Solutions, success extended beyond providing payroll and accounting services. Their team of professionals actively engaged with clients, offering advice, guidance, and strategic insights to drive business growth. They conduct regular processing reviews, identify potential cost-saving measures, and recommend improvements in payroll processes.

CADJPro Payroll Solutions has become a trusted partner, empowering businesses to thrive in an increasingly competitive market.

Fueling Growth and Expansion

As word spread about the exceptional services provided by CADJPro Payroll Solutions, the company experienced exponential growth. Their reputation for reliability and professionalism attracted businesses from various industries, allowing CADJPro Payroll Solutions to expand their reach and impact.

The firm's commitment to excellence and unwavering dedication to client success propelled them to become a leader in the payroll and accounting industry for small businesses.

Conclusion

Garcia and CADJPRO Payroll Solutions have established themselves as a beacon of support and upliftment for small businesses in Canada. By offering tailored payroll solutions, streamlining processes, ensuring compliance, and providing expert guidance, Garcia has transformed the lives of countless entrepreneurs and employees.

Through her commitment to accuracy, data security, and nurturing client relationships, she has uplifted businesses, allowing them to thrive and flourish. CADJPRO Payroll Solutions stands as a testament to the power of dedication, innovation, and empathy in contributing to the upliftment of companies and individuals.

Garcia Hanson-Francis, CPM

CADJPro Payroll Solutions - Empowering Your Business with Exceptional Payroll and Accounting Services.Garcia Hanson-Francis - A Passionate Payroll Leadership Professional.

Are you a small business owner in need of specialized accounting and payroll solutions? Look no further! Meet Garcia Hanson-Francis, the owner of CADJPro Payroll Solutions, a boutique payroll and accounting firm dedicated to providing effective, comprehensive, and personalized services.

Garcia's journey into the world of payroll and accounting was born out of personal struggles. Having faced financial challenges in the past and experiencing confusion with payroll in previous roles, Garcia understands the importance of simplifying the complexities of financial management. With a mission to alleviate stress and streamline processes for small businesses, Garcia became a Certified Payroll Manager and founded CADJPro Payroll Solutions.

What sets Garcia apart is her genuine passion for supporting businesses in achieving success. With over 20 years of experience in payroll, Garcia's expertise is unrivalled. She is a QuickBooks Pro Advisor and holds certifications in Business Writing and various accounting disciplines.

Her book, "*Blessed by God, Broken by Life, A Payroll Leadership Professional,*" showcases her dedication to sharing insights and knowledge with others.

Beyond her role at CADJPro, Garcia is a founding member of Immigrant Women in Business (IWB) and actively champions the support of female entrepreneurs. She serves as a mentor to new business owners and recruits female volunteers seeking to gain expertise in the field. Garcia's commitment to fostering growth and empowerment within the community is truly inspiring.

One of Garcia's notable accomplishments is winning the *People's Choice Awards* in the Accountant category three years in a row. This recognition speaks volumes about her exceptional skills, work ethic, and dedication to client satisfaction.

In addition to her professional achievements, Garcia runs the CADJPro Virtual Tax Clinic, a platform through which she prepares tax returns for underprivileged populations, including seniors, immigrants, students, incarcerated individuals, and single families. This initiative reflects Garcia's compassion and commitment to making a positive impact on the lives of others.

When working with Garcia, you can expect an engaging and collaborative experience. Her good gut instincts, polite nature, and ability to have complex discussions make her a pleasure to work with. With a strong focus on planning and implementation, Garcia is results-oriented and dedicated to helping you achieve your business goals.

If you're ready to experience the transformative power of expert payroll and accounting services, partner with CADJPro Payroll Solutions and benefit from Garcia Hanson-Francis' wealth of knowledge and unwavering commitment to your success.

Contact Garcia Hanson-Francis today at www.cadjpro.com and take the first step towards empowering your business with the best in payroll and accounting expertise.

WHAT DOES IT MEAN TO BE AN ENTREPRENEUR, AND WHY DO I WANT TO BE ONE?

Josef D Stetter

Being an entrepreneur does not mean running a Fortune 100 company right away, which ironically scares most people away from even trying; it simply means you are doing something that generates additional income and ignites your passion. The truth is that there are many entrepreneurs that struggle at first, and this is why having mentors and a tribe or mastermind to help you see things from different angles is so important. Both a mentor and a mastermind will offer ideas that you might not think of on your own, introductions to people that can become clients, vendors, suppliers and/or strategic partners that will help elevate and grow your business faster and easier!

There is a myriad of opportunities that exist more than ever. People today can work from home with little more than a computer and an internet connection and bring in a steady income. Some side hustles include: playing video games, drop shipping, content creation on social media, graphic design, video editing, animation, translation, writing and editing, voice-over, tutoring, teaching (music, art, crafts, video game playing, programming, cooking and many more). Two great resources to see how others monetize their genius are https://www.fiverr.com/ and https://www.upwork.com/. So, hopefully, it is clear that opportunities exist everywhere!

The truth is that job security DOES NOT exist anymore! The pandemic proved this as 65 million people lost their job in North America. Many of us recognize the importance of having a backup plan, or a "side gig," which can become a higher income than your typical 9 to 5 job. Getting a career to finance your passion is responsible and allows you to learn and gain experience. Please choose something that you enjoy, not just a good-paying job. In case you were never told JOB means 'just over broke' or 'Journey of the broke,' or "Just Obey your Boss.' Do you notice a pattern? A job is chasing money, while a career is following a passion. Mark Twain said, *"Find a job you enjoy doing, and you will never have to work a day in your life."*

Being an entrepreneur is having the freedom of choice and time in life. It's evolved to mean much more than a way to make money in modern society. To speak of an entrepreneur is to speak of a person who is both creative and resourceful enough to recognize a gap in the market and the opportunity it presents. Anyone, regardless of age, education, or background, may be an entrepreneur. Their unique qualities include originality, imagination, and a strong will to succeed. While there are benefits to working alone, being an entrepreneur does not necessitate doing so. It is impossible for a single person to survive on this planet by themself. To put it another way, we can't make it without each other's support. This rule applies to absolutely everyone. Who do you rely on if you are a sole proprietor, a partnership, or a corporation? Customers! You still need other people's help, even if your business is small enough that you can manage it on your own. The wonderful thing is no matter what you want to offer that improves or innovates or offers something new, you can be certain there is a market for it, and people around the world that will buy it. So, being an entrepreneur gives you more freedom and choice, especially once you have solved the kinks and learned what is needed to grow the business. Until you do, having a career you enjoy that pays the bills and finances your dreams is a way to get the best of both worlds.

Now let's explore what is the right business for you — otherwise referred to as your WHY.

Your WHY is that one or two things that excite you, that ignites you, or that gives you a purpose bigger than yourself. For some, it's their family or the opportunity to give them a better life and generational wealth; for others, it is raising awareness and resources for a specific issue or cause, such as a disease. Some are driven by leaving a legacy and making an impact on the world to make it a better place. A WHY can be to honour someone who has passed, suffered or benefited from you in their life; A WHY can be helping the environment. There is no one WHY or right WHY; there is the one or two that make you feel alive and excited. HINT: Money is not the WHY but rather what you can do and who you can help with the money. In other words: it is the result of making a difference and impacting others. HINT: The more you can serve others, the bigger your WHY and the more opportunities you will have as an entrepreneur. To help you find your WHY, try doing some of the following exercises:

Exercise 1: List of 100. A timer will go off in five minutes, and you'll have to do this activity as quickly as possible. This is meant to be a free-flowing mental workout. The subject of your list is up to you. Here are a few lists you can create: There are a hundred things I want to accomplish in my lifetime, one hundred things I wish I hadn't said or done, one hundred people I want to reconnect with, one hundred things I would do if I had an infinite amount of money, a hundred things I enjoy, a hundred things I hate and so on. While it's up to you, I would suggest covering a wide range of possibilities. It's fine to include the same things twice on your list. Two of my closest friends and I did this activity together, and then we compared notes. To put it mildly, the findings were eye-opening. You'll start to see recurring themes once you've passed the 50th spot and are into the last 50. There will be a dominant tendency (or two) that you keep listing, even if you express thoughts in different ways and use different terms. Pull together a quick summary using the most often mentioned points from your list. This will help you better understand who you are and what you are about as part of discovering your WHY.

Another great exercise is to envision yourself discovering a time capsule buried by your family in the backyard of your childhood home. Given the passage of time, you no longer remember what was in the secret compartment. You discover a letter written by your younger self as a gift. You, as a young person, are solely interested in knowing how things ended out for you today, namely, where you are, how you got here, and what choices you made that led you here. Answer your own letter. If you want to get in touch with someone from your past or present, you can use this letter-writing prompt to do it. It has amazing curative properties. If you're having trouble letting go of the past, possibly because of a relationship that ended unexpectedly and has left you confused and yearning for an explanation, but you can't find one because the other person is no longer in your life, then this article is for you. Maybe they've moved on, but it's still a bad idea to contact them. Why not give writing a try? You, the author, could either be posing or responding to the queries. Given that this message is intended solely for your eyes, feel free to ask anything you desire; nothing is off-limits. You will find patterns in what you need answered in your letters. They will get you closer to your "Why."

The third exercise to find your WHY: Create your own death notice or obituary. We are aware of the significance of drafting a Will. The act of making things easier for your loved ones after you die is seen as a responsible one. A similar point can be made about penning your obituary. Writing an obituary for a loved one is a difficult undertaking, as anyone will attest who has been given this responsibility. I encourage you to put pen to paper and create your own personal goodbye letter as a gift to your loved ones. Tell me how it reads. How content are you with your accomplishments? Do you find it difficult to compose even a single paragraph? If this is the case, go ahead and compose the eulogy of your dreams. Take risks, think big, and don't hold back. However, you must tell the truth. My friend, how do you wish to be remembered? Here is the potential ground for a revolutionary change to take place. The "Why" you do what you do is also embedded there. Now that you know your "Why," what are you going to do with that knowledge? If you've done the activities, you should be able to identify your "Why." It may be a [blank], so that [blank] statement, but it's not required. You can answer this question with a single word, an expression, a sentence, or even a whole paragraph.

For what reasons did you set out to discover your "Why"? Because we intend to take advantage of it. Getting in touch with your personal "Why" is essential to achieving your personal best. Just be, take a deep breath, and let your "Why" guide you. The time has come to start the metamorphosis. Everyone is changeable, despite widespread belief to the contrary. The only thing we can bank on is that things will change. Things are always evolving, so it's possible that you'll need to revise your WHY statement as time goes on. Nonetheless, I agree that your initial "Why" statement is the one that best reflects who you are at your heart and will serve as your compass through the many challenges that "change" always brings. Doing what you love because It matters is how to live the most purposeful life! The decision is entirely up to you. Either get out there and start living or sit around on the sidelines and settle for a mediocre existence. The sad reality is that 80-90% of people in North America HATE their job. Think about that, most people hate what they do and NEVER change this because they are too afraid! The rest of us need you, so please stay among the living. Discover your "Why," and you'll find the unrestrained joy that comes from helping others for no other reason than it makes you feel good, and you can.

So, who am I, to offer this advice? My name is Josef Stetter, and I had to switch careers 9x and jobs over 18X to discover my WHY and my love for entrepreneurship. Along the way, I started helping people land their dream job now and companies to hire the right fit people and keep them for their organizations. Every time I get an opportunity to share my wisdom on job finding, career changes and corporate culture, I light up with excitement.

Thus far, I have helped over 11,000 people and have done so in as little as two days. This is part of my WHY, to help over a million people land their dream job now. The other part of my WHY is my beautiful children and wife, that inspire me, encourage me, and always make me laugh.

I had a business partner that taught me life lessons that cost me over $330,000 and derailed my passion and purpose for nearly ten years. I stopped letting my light shine and being an entrepreneur that wanted to make the world a better place and was miserable and lost until I met my incredible wife.

I found the right mentors and the right masterminds, and now, I am expanding my horizons and my interest in various entrepreneurship opportunities as I can help more people and show my family that anything is possible. That is why I created a program that offers people all the tools, resources, systems and tricks to help all job seekers get hired faster and easier.

https://www.landyourdreamjobnow.com/. If you need me to help your company to hire the right people and help with the corporate culture, reach out to the Celebrate Group.

Josef D Stetter

For over 16 years, Josef Stetter has incorporated humour, energy, passion and full self-expression into his personal and professional life.

Award-Winning and International Best-Selling Author of Canada *Congratulations You Are Hired*: *It Was Easier Than You Thought* and USA Congratulations *You Are Hired: It Was Easier Than You Thought*. Published four other books.

Award-Winning Speaker and Guinness World Record participant

Didn't know what he wanted to do when he grew up, so switched careers 9 X and jobs 17 times

Works in Recruitment. Clients have included: Deloitte & Touche, Aecon Construction, Tata Consulting Services, Canon, Aviva, Skechers Shoes and more!

Personally, helped over 11,000 find a job they love with a 90% success rate of finding anyone employment in any field in under three months with proven systems. The fastest he helped people land a great role is in two days.

Josef Stetter brings forth an interesting twist to getting things done and achieving results that go well beyond expectations.

Josef Stetter helps you take the headache out of navigating the abyss of job searching or hiring by sharing advanced strategies that maximize results. He understands the importance of clear, concise, confident and conversational communication to generate results that are truly unbelievable!!!

Follow him on Instagram

https://www.instagram.com/josef_stetter/

About *Land Your Dream Job*

He understands the job market very well while connecting people to their purpose and identifying the right opportunities -- whether advertised on a job board or knowing what's going on inside the hidden job market.

He changed careers nine times and had a multitude of jobs, so he understands your frustration when it comes to proving your transferable skills. Invested $25,000 to master the psychology of job finding and has systems and tools that Guarantee Results.

As a career coach and job market advisor for two decades, he's written several books on the subject matter, has assisted thousands of people land their dream job and continues to support people with valuable resources and tools.

Become a member of his Facebook Group - LAND YOUR DREAM JOB - at:

https://www.facebook.com/groups/Landyourdreamjob2020/ and get a free copy of *SECRETS TO YOUR DREAM JOB REVEALED!*

This program is definitely for you if you're feeling:

· Anxious from job loss due to Covid-19

· Frustrated with the lack of response to your job applications · 'Overqualified'

· Frustrated that you haven't gotten the job you really want

· Unhappy with your current employer

· Ready for a career change

The Land Your Dream Job program has 8 Modules plus bonus modules. There is a pre-recorded Video and Audio. There is a

PowerPoint slide deck for each unit; there are also PDF files of resources that include templates, research on where to network, top agencies in Canada and the USA, explaining the psychology of interviewing, questions candidates can ask an interviewer, top job finding sites and more.

He is booking numerous interviews on Podcasts and radio shows throughout Canada and USA to build traction and awareness and draw traffic to the program. He is also holding webinars; the first one was November 24, 2020.

These are some of the useful tips and tools you will learn from his program:

1. Secrets about the Applicant Tracking System and how the algorithms score your resume & Getting responses from online applications

2. RESUMES that get noticed

3. How to WOW the interviewer

4. Optimizing Your Job Search – LinkedIn, Networking & Referrals

5. Creative job-finding strategies

6. Working with recruiters/agencies and getting interviews

7. Salary negotiations

8. Creating a position just for you that does not exist

AND SO MANY BONUSES!!

Course: https://www.landyourdreamjobnow.com/

Instagram: https://www.instagram.com/josef_stetter

LinkedIn: https://www.linkedin.com/in/josefstetter

Gmail: landyourdreamjobnow@gmail.com

TikTok: @landyourdreamjob_now

About the Celebrate Group

We at The Celebrate Group understand corporate culture and the importance of team unity. Thus, we become part of your team as Corporate Culturalists, providing clear and creative solutions to excite and engage your staff, thereby increasing your company's productivity by a minimum of 25%. We promote the right kind of corporate culture by increasing hiring efficiencies when we find the right candidates at the right time, using in-depth analysis, understanding the skills required while leveraging vast networks, both online and offline. We combine our sourcing strategies with high-level psychological, personality and value assessments to ensure the highest level of compatibility between the company, as well as the candidates' needs.

Let's start the conversation and see the possibilities unfold!

www.celebrategroup.ca

WHAT COLLABORATION MEANS TO ME

Alan Wade

I have learned many things over the years. Some of those lessons were very important to learn. Experiencing some of those lessons was not that good at the time, but as I look back on my life, I realize every experience I had turned out to be all good. You can look back at your life and see it with anger or sadness, or just perhaps you can see it for what it truly was — steppingstones to where you are today. Every event in my life, whether it was a very traumatic event, failed relationships, or loss of family or friends, has made me one of the most resilient people you will ever meet. It is all in how you look at it.

Some of the most important lessons I have learned over the years is to ask for help. Accept help when someone offers it to you. Collaborating with others is one of the best ways to learn from others and to get help from others. I have collaborated with Robert many times on many different books. That opened the doors to collaborating with many other people on many other books and projects. Every time I collaborated with someone, I got to see things from different perspectives. I learned different skills.

Success to me most likely means something totally different than it means to someone else. It is obvious we all see the world from different perspectives. That is the beauty of this world. My values, attitudes, and beliefs are mine and mine alone. Yes, someone may have the same values and, yes, even beliefs and attitudes, but that does not mean they are exactly the same as mine are. I have been honoured to be able to work with many, many other people. This alone has helped and moulded me to become and better teacher and person. What is my definition of success, you may ask? What the real question should be is, what do I value? What are my beliefs? What is my attitude?

What do I value? This sounds like such a simple question, but of course, if you ask this question, you will end up with many other questions to answer. Simply put, I value family first. My wife and kids are what I value the most. I would do anything for them. My extended family, aunts, uncles, cousins, nephews, nieces, and friends are all included. I am the type of person that shows love by doing things for family and friends and, yes, other people. I am an action-type personality. My actions speak louder than my words. I value helping people, whether it is someone I know or may have just met.

My attitude is quite a simple one. I treat others the way I want to be treated. I do the things I do — not for money, fame, or recognition. I do these things so that at the end of the day when I am ready to sleep, I know I have been the best version of myself. I am not in competition with anyone else. The only person I am in competition with is myself. Yes, this sounds strange, but I want to be better and get better every day. What I teach people is to do the things you do but with no expectations. Yes, open that door for someone, and if they do not say thank you, who cares? I did it because I wanted to do it. This is my attitude.

My beliefs are much in line with my values and attitudes. I believe people deserve to have the happiness they are looking for or whatever it is they are looking for. I also believe that collaborating with others helps me and the people in my life. It also helps the people I am working with and supporting. Something I had to work on changing was my limiting beliefs. When I was young, I learned that anger was how you dealt with things that happened in your life. Changing limiting beliefs is not what I help others to do virtually every day now. Think about this when we work with someone else, we have help from a different perspective. We also get the experiences of the other person to help us as well. These are just some of the reasons I have done so many collaborations with other people.

My definition of success is quite simple. I am all about family and friends. I have done many personality tests, and they all come out as nurturer, action, research, and blueprint-type personality. Nurturer I like to help my family and friends as well as my clients. I like to empower people and lift them up to realize they are more than they think they are. I like to act when an opportunity comes up; it does not take me long to decide. I am ok with doing some research on subjects or things. The one thing I am not that good at is following a system or method of doing things unless the system works for everyone.

Where I worked for years, it was all about the organization, not helping the people it was supposed to be supporting. A community organization should be all about the people it works for. So, I had to do something or, should I say, break some rules and put the client's needs first. So, success to me is the ability to stay true to my beliefs, to my personality, and to do the things I love to do.

I have learned so many things from working with Robert and all the other people I have been lucky enough to collaborate with. As I have said before, collaborating with others has helped me see things from a different perspective. This alone has helped me to grow and expand myself to a higher level of awareness and understanding. When I became an addiction counsellor could never have imagined becoming a ten-time International Best-Selling Author.

Virtually everything I have succeeded in doing and the person I have become was directly because I collaborated with someone else. It goes like this I collaborated with my partner to write our first book *The Magic Within: How to Transform Your Life.* That book transformed our lives, and clients came to us for help. That book was directly responsible for the creation of *The Magic Within Coaching and Consulting Company.* Up to the time before we wrote our first book, I had no interest in writing books. After our first book, I got the chance to collaborate with Robert J Moore on Magnetic Entrepreneur; it was a success.

That led to working directly and collaborating with Robert on our book *Awakening: Out of the Darkness Into The Light.* This book is a detailed story of two men overcoming terrible traumatic events in their lives to become two totally different people from whom they started out to be. This book led to more public speaking events where my personal story helped others to change their lives. So, I think you are beginning to see the picture that collaborating with one person may lead to working with another person and another.

Collaborating has opened so many doors I could never have imagined in my wildest dreams. It all started with my first collaboration with my soon-to-be wife, Cindy Preston. So, I must thank everyone I have collaborated with over the years. I will just use first names to make it easier, Cindy, Ray, Robert J Moore, Scott, Tom, Michael, Les, Alain, Matt, John, Caroline, and many others as well. As I started the last sentence, I realized that there are so many collaborations I have forgotten many of them. I must apologize to the others.

Alan Wade

Alan Wade is a Ten-Time International Best-Selling Author, Guinness World Record participant, Certified Master Practitioner of NLP, Hypnotherapy MER®, and NLP Life Coach, Reiki Master, Social Service Worker with a Native Specialization, Founder and Lead Coach at *The Magic Within Coaching, and Consulting Company*, Public Speaker, however, these are all just titles.

My greatest achievements have been becoming a better person and learning to be more patient and understanding. Being able to let go of the terrible trauma that ruled my life for seventeen or so years was an amazing benefit.

What he is most proud of is being a father and dad and being a better partner and soon-to-be husband. You can connect with him at www.tmw.coach, by email at tmw.coach@gmail.com, call or text at 705 698 2437.

The Secret to Incredible Sales Videos: Why Should They Care?

Jim Beard

IT'S NOT ABOUT YOU.

Take a minute. Breathe.

I know that you think of your product or service like your baby, and when people don't buy that, it's like them saying you have an ugly baby. You have put your heart and soul into making it absolutely amazing and life-changing.

M:

Have you ever had a friend that was constantly telling you how incredible, smart, talented, etc., their child is? It's exhausting and BORING. We don't care. Congrats on your super baby, but I have things to do today. Somehow we think our business is different.

It's easy to fall into the trap of talking about only OUR journey in our scripts as it is OUR experience, and we want to use it to show others that we know what we are talking about, but THEY DON'T CARE. Think about how you view it when someone goes on and on about themselves. You zone out, and if you can, you leave the conversation. This is even worse online, where the average attention span is less every year.

Meet them where THEY ARE and meet THEIR needs, and you will have their attention. Don't make them look up at you on the mountain shouting down at them, telling them to come on up. They need to mirror themselves in your experience and journey to see it is possible and that you are the person or business that can get them there. Service is connecting your passion to someone else's need. The problem comes in when we only focus on OUR passion and not the customer or audience's NEED.

A:

Video Marketing and sales aren't going anywhere. According to Wyzowl Research, 86% of businesses now use some form of video marketing.

94% of businesses say they plan to continue using video marketing over the next 12 months and forward.

84% say they made a purchase after watching a brand's video.

69% actually prefer video when learning about a product or service.

Audiences are TWICE as likely to share video content with their peers.

Marketers feel more positive about video's return on investment than at any point since 2015, as they report an unprecedented level of influence on KPIs such as traffic, leads, sales, and audience understanding.

More marketers credited video with increasing dwell time, traffic, leads, sales, and reduced support queries than in ANY of the annual surveys since 2015, - while an all-time high number of marketers (92%) stated they get a good ROI on video content, up from 87% in 2022.

It's more important than ever to get video marketing right, or you will be left behind by the rest of the world. But don't worry, I've got you covered. Take a step back from the ledge.

Here are the Secrets To Ensure Your Audience Will Actually Care About Your Video Content, get you noticed by the right audience and surprise and delight them so they become raving fans and lasting customers.

V:

WHO is the video for? Think about your target audience.

Clarify your target audience

Formulate a value proposition to meet the needs of the AUDIENCE

Write down what you do

Why do you like it?

What makes YOU care about it?

How do you want people to feel after watching your video?

General Example: You love seeing your pet happy and excited. Your pet loves going for walks, and it makes them very happy. You grab the leash and go for a walk with your pet. Passion meets need.

The problem comes in when our pet is hungry, but we still grab the leash. The passion and need no longer line up.

Business Example: You love helping people to find paths through their trauma using your experience from your own trauma. They need a guide that knows what they are going through and how to overcome it. You create a program that meets their need and helps them to overcome their past trauma and move forward in their life on a path towards their personal happiness. Passion meets need.

The problem comes in when we only focus on our own trauma journey and what worked for us rather than customizing the experience to the individual. The passion and need no longer work together.

NO ONE CARES about you or your product or service until you Make Them CARE.

How to find out what THEY WANT and GIVE IT TO THEM.

Make a List of all of the reasons they should care.

Start with Youtube. Type in the keywords associated with your product or service. Check the videos that have the most views. Skip watching the video and go right to the comments. If the comments are saying they wished that "blank" was covered or that the video did a bad job at "blank," write it down. If the comments are all saying the video was insanely good, watch the video and take notes.

Filter through the list and determine the top 5 reasons why they should care.

Cut the list down to the BIG MAIN REASON or two reasons they should care. These will be the foundation on which your messaging will be built.

Give real value that THEY NEED and will help them now. Pretty simple here. No fake value or disguising our sales message as value that won't actually help.

Stories help the audience/customer to see themselves in your product or service. You and your audience need to desire the same thing. The difference is your solution works, and you can prove it, which is different from what they have tried.

Customers buy emotionally and rationalize logically. Always think in terms of Towards pleasure or Away from pain. You are their guide, and they are the hero. It is easy to fall into the habit of us being the hero, and then they want to follow the hero. That is NOT the case. I call this the Lambo Method. It's where people show how successful they are and how unsuccessful the viewer is. This works for like 4 seconds and makes the viewer feel inadequate/bad. In the best videos, You are taking them towards pleasure or taking them away from their current pain on their path to becoming the hero. You are just supporting them.

Example of Format to Keep in Mind: Weakness, Goal, Transformation, Support. We show them a weakness we had, what our goal was, how we overcame it and how the viewer can too.

The audience wants something new. It can be a spin on something they already know, but it should have a fresh perspective or angle that it uses to address the problem.

General Example: Janitor or Master of the Custodial Arts

Business Example: Mindset Coaching or Peak Performance Transformation Coaching

Consistency in messaging and branding from ad/post through the Call to Action.

Make sure that your messaging and branding are the same throughout. If they click on an ad promising a 10X improvement in their conversions and the landing page looks different and talks only about the power of organic content, there is a mismatch. They are coming for the conversions, not extra work in making organic content.

Example of how to make it work: Ad: You Are One Of A Kind. Why Is Your Facial Cream Made For EVERYONE? Landing Page Headline: A Custom Bottle For Your Dark Spots, And No One Else's. Sub Headline: Get Glowing Skin With A Powerful Cream Mixed Just For You.

S:

Use these methods, and I know that your videos will make more connections, fans, and of course, BUYERS. A great way to gauge the success of your new-found video skills that will improve your future videos is to Ask Others to Review It and Ask Them If They Will BUY, NOT if They Like It.

Your Aunt Gertrude Loves It. She Won't Buy.

T:

I personally have used these methods to help my clients generate nearly 6 million dollars with their products or services. VIDEOS WORK. If they aren't working, it is USER ERROR. You need a different approach, and now you have a winning approach. And don't give up after one video doesn't kill it. It takes trial and error.

Even the best-performing videos take a little bit of tweaking for them to really knock it out of the park. I had a client that had a Video Sales Letter that wasn't performing. I tweaked it about four times until we nailed it. In his particular case, his audience didn't like his hook, so after we changed it, the video took off.

C:

I Challenge you to use these techniques in your business starting TODAY and watch your conversions skyrocket. I mean it. Your videos will be "Fire," as the kids say. This method has helped countless entrepreneurs to get their brands in front of their ideal audience and form raving fans that can't wait to buy from you, knowing that your brand equals trust and confidence.

Are you making your first video yet?

Seriously, GO. You've got this. Start with your phone for now, and then upgrade your gear as you go along. You don't need to be Spielberg to create great sales videos. You just need to remember the very most important thing. THEM (The Audience). They are all that matters. They are the ones that need your help. They are the ones that pay you.

G:

I can guarantee that if you DON'T take advantage of these tips that, your product, service, or brand will go the way of the dinosaurs. EXTINCT. *Cue Jurassic Park Theme Song* Don't be like the dinosaurs when you can thrive in this new landscape and reap the benefits while your competitors are still struggling to figure out where to start with video.

B:

Added Bonus:

In addition to this section, I have also given you a great script format to follow for your sales videos. You will notice these small letters above before paragraph text, so you can see how I utilized this format in the writing of this chapter.

The format is:

H/Hook where we capture their attention

M/Mirror or allow the audience to mirror themselves in your story

A/Authority Building, where we demonstrate our own competence or the value of the info and let them know we can help

V/Value or deliver on the reason they are watching the video

S/Soft CTA, where we let them know what is coming and how we can help

T/Testimonials to show them there have been others that came before them and had success

C/Call to Action (CTA), where we show them an opportunity to take their pain away or show them a path toward their better future

G/Guarantee where we reduce their risk from taking a chance on us

B/Bonus where we give added incentive to take action

Now get out there and make better videos for THEM, because that is why we do it all anyways, to help THEM.

"I don't expect success. I prepare for it." ~ Ryan Reynolds

Best To You

Jim Beard

Love & Leads Founder

Social Media/Contact Info

Facebook: https://www.facebook.com/jim.beard.micromachine/

Website: LoveandLeads.com

Rise, Fall, Rising

Joseph Loney

I was deeply appreciative and thankful to the staff, a genuine sense of gratitude; what I had in my possession twenty hours earlier was all handed back to me; they had treated me with dignity and a great deal of respect.

I had signed for it whilst being booked in, and now, signing for its safe return to me.

It didn't amount to much, at 54 years of age, a wallet that I had purchased in South Korea many years before. I treasured that wallet; the contents were of no significance to me these days; a bank card was useless as there was little or no money in the bank to use, my driving licence, well at least that's some form of ID, if I was ever found if I ever carried out the actions, that were hitting me like relentless waves and had been torturing me for the past several months. Bless them; they had charged my iPhone whilst I was being assessed; at least I had some juice in the phone, tobacco, papers, a translucent green disposable lighter, and my khaki green winter coat.

I was relieved to see the tobacco; I so wanted a cigarette. Earlier that morning, I'd asked and was given an electronic cigarette to use. It tasted of plastic and felt so false, similar to the cup of tea that had been served in a plastic beaker with no handle.

I was grateful to have a warm drink as I sat assessing the cell that I was inhabiting, pacing the secure room; I was reminded of prison movies I had watched. Should I set about doing some push-ups like they do in those films, use the time wisely and constructively? Tiredness was enveloping my whole body, I'd been sleeping roughly for several days, and whilst last night I had a bed to sleep in, I had been disturbed every fifteen minutes by a member of staff opening the spy hole in the security door and shining a torch into the cell to check on me.

The floor, walls and ceiling all seemed to be one, with no joins, no way to decipher where one stopped and one started, a pale light blue door, like the cup, it had no handle. The hinges were hidden within the door, and the viewing glass was opaque and distorted the corridor outside, like viewing life through the bottom of a glass bottle, and this door could only be opened from the other side.

There was some paperwork to sign, not reading the content of each document; I scribbled my name several times and was handed an official small document to keep; I read the first few lines.

Reasons why you have been detained under the Mental Health Act,

I read no more; I knew why and thought to myself, well, at least I have proof that I was sectioned, locked up in a secure unit, for my own safety, folded neatly, it went into the top pocket of my coat. Pressing the press stud hard to ensure it wouldn't escape, and with no intention of ever showing that letter to anyone, there it could stay.

As I fastened my brown leather belt, It dawned on me as to how much weight I had lost recently; feeling embarrassed, I pulled the belt as tight as possible. I was ready, ready to leave; once more my personal belongings were checked, I had everything I had come in with.

With each security door, being unlocked, I was stepping closer to the outside world again. It felt good to be leaving this sterile environment; as the outer door was unlocked, it hit me, hit me very hard; what was I going out to?

Still within the main hospital grounds, and out of the corner of my eye, I spotted the staff bicycle store, metal framed, with plastic sheets forming the roof. Fine drizzling rain and grey clouds, it was the end of a cold January day.

I made my way over to the bike shelter, shaking and reaching deep into my left pocket, tobacco and papers, gently balancing the pouch of tobacco on a bicycle saddle, chained and padlocked to the cold steel frame.

My fingers were stained yellow from the previous days' chain-smoking; my body was aching; last night's bed had been hard and uncomfortable. As I rolled the cigarette, digging deep into my coat pocket, I located my lighter by touch and lit the tightly rolled cigarette now delicately being held between my lips.

It gave me a sense of space and time to gather my senses and thoughts; nothing mattered right then in that moment, drawing on the diminishing cigarette; this was valuable time.

My phone was fully charged, yet I didn't want to use it. I feared draining the battery and had no place to charge it, but I needed to check my messages, who had been trying to reach me, my son, he knew where I was, and check what money I had in the bank.

Opening the bank app sent a wave of fear that cut right through me, £14 – at least I was in credit. Twenty-four ago, I'd had over £50 and in the space of a few short hours, I'd spent 30 quid on booze and a pub burger, squandering the little money I had and undoing 24 years of sobriety. Occasionally I'd thought and often been asked how much it would take to get me drunk. In my mind, I backtracked to yesterday, five, maybe six beers. Was I mad?

I needed a taxi and googled local firms; only then it dawned on me that I had no destination; where would I be going? To gather my thoughts and senses, I rolled another smoke; you have nowhere to go; the words were on a continual loop in my head.

Rock bottom again, end of the road. Come on, Joe, I said to myself, repeating some positive thoughts; yeah, this is a bad place to be; you're strong, you're resilient, you can do this, you have to do this.

Several months previously, I had hit what I believed to be my rock bottom, yet here I was, cold, wet, homeless and alone, my mind racing at 100 mph, trying to work out, figure out what was next. Daylight was fading, and I squatted down in the bike shelter for that moment in time. It was my sanctuary,

In an effort to figure things out, my mind wandered back to different times in my life, like clouds in the sky on a bright sunny day. My past life came into my thoughts and went out again; occasionally, a glimpse of the past would freeze in my mind's eye, moments in time I was happy to recall, and others that I simply wanted to never see or experience again.

As part of my release from the unit, it was arranged for me to meet with an emergency housing officer the following morning. It was a beacon of light, but it was tomorrow; my immediate problem was the next 12-16 hours.

I'm actually homeless; I kept telling myself; it was relentless; the same words kept repeating in my head, as though the more I said it and listened to it, I would find the answer!

For the next ten to fifteen minutes, I felt elevated from my physical body; two scenes were playing out in my mind's eye.

I was watching myself, sitting in the bicycle shed, as though the real-life movie of my life to date was being played in front of me, my gaunt, bearded face staring back at my higher self, I was watching me, and I was watching the movie.

Not one other single thought entered my mind; it was a cinematic, out-of-body experience. The dishevelled me was transfixed, unable to control the visual lifetime experiences; the elevated me was watching both unfold, gauging any flicker of reaction. I was reliving, viewing my life in that spacious moment of time.

Was it a way of making sense of it all? If you pay attention to the patterns of your life, you realize everything always works out. My elevated state knew that the man in the bicycle shed was full of fear. I'd been living full-on with fear for months, and how the hell was this going to work for my greater good?

Flicking from one life event to the next, then rewinding, replaying, as hard as I tried, I could not stop the movie loop from playing. Maybe I could take a different route, make a better decision and change the course of the past. My higher self knew that this was impossible and that the process I was in was a cathartic one; it needed to happen. Right at that moment, I was both the actor and the witness, and to move forward, the witness needed to be dominant.

I was a father to two beautiful children, born ten years apart, and to different mothers, they truly are my world, but over the last year, I had become distant from them, wrapped up in my world of despair and fear, every aspect of my once beautiful existence had fallen off the cliff edge, and my relationship with both my children had suffered.

It was now a dark, rain-soaked evening; the street lighting gave a sense of warmth. The movie was still playing in my mind, watching me relive the decision to end my life. I'd gone through some crazy scenarios as to how — which way would guarantee the outcome that I'd convinced myself was the best way to rid myself of not only physical but desperate mental pain. Methodically and almost military-like, the plan was worked out. Taking a towel from my small supply of personal effects and cutting it in half to create two equal lengths, I made a noose and tied it to the shower rail in my bathroom. Sitting on the floor, I had spent hours looking at my handy work, going through the scenarios of when I was dicing with death and even practised putting it around my neck, my legs out in front of me. All I needed was to let my feet slip forward, and I would be slipping into unconsciousness. Before I carried out the act, I wanted to write to my children and loved ones. I apologized, expressing my deepest unconditional love for them, how I reached the end of my road and that I had nothing left to offer.

I awoke the next morning, handwritten desperate notes strewn across my bed and the noose still in place in the shower. I'd hoped that the morning would bring a new sense of belief within myself, a night of good sleep and the hope that my current situation would have disappeared.

A sense of guilt rushed through my body as I re-read the notes to my children; was it desperation, selfishness? Complete hopelessness had taken over once again; I drew the curtains to block out the sunlight that was filling my bedroom and, for a moment, thought about how long it would be before I would be discovered.

Maybe the drawn curtains would raise suspicion among the neighbours. This is it; today, right now, I scanned the room, placing the notes neatly at the foot of the bed, knowing that when the door gets broken in, they'll find the notes before finding me, and that will give whomever it is the heads up, as to what they'll discover next.

Staff from the secure unit were now leaving after their day's work; it was early evening, and the bike shelter was quickly empty of bikes. Tim, who had been one of the six psychiatrists assessing me a few hours previously, quietly and discreetly unchained his bicycle and wished me the best of luck. "You're a resilient guy, Joe; you can turn this situation around; I truly believe that, Joe.

His words were genuine, and I could sense kindness in his tone, and for a fleeting moment, he had created an interval in my movie. "But Joe, you can't stay here in this area for much longer; hospital security have you on CCTV and will be escorting you off the grounds, take care Joe."

With those words circulating in my head, I reflected on the assessment, being escorted finally into a large room with secure glazed windows looking out onto an unkempt green area within the secure facility.

Six psychiatrists sat in a horseshoe arrangement, Tim was directly in front of me, and he facilitated the assessment. This was my chance to convince them that I was insane, an opportunity to get the help I so desperately wanted; I would have to act it up a lot and put on a show.

Did I want to be held in this type of unit? I wanted help, but was this the place for me? I considered Jack Nicholson in *One Flew Over the Cuckoo's Nest* and how he had to act out his insanity to get moved from prison to the hospital.

As the assessment unfolded, the real true authentic me shone through; I didn't wish to put on an act. This was a serious situation, and I could do nothing more than be me. My eye contact was good; I looked back at whoever asked the question and engaged with them directly,

Tim, ran through as to why I had been brought into the unit, and he thanked me for being compliable with the process and the staff.

"Joe, your son, contacted the police yesterday early afternoon; as we understand it, you've been going through a crisis in recent months. He was extremely concerned for your welfare, knowing that you've been living in your vehicle for the last few days and that yesterday, you made reference to wanting to end your life.

The police found you in a pub, and you had been drinking. We believe that you have been alcohol-free for over 20 years, so a decision was made to detain you, and you freely came here with the police to be admitted."

"What can you tell us about what's been going on for you, Joe?"

At this moment, I pondered my truth; I wanted help, and I didn't want to be locked up.

I addressed Tim directly but also engaged in eye contact with the others,

"I've had a wonderful life, Tim, yes, it's been full of ups and downs, traumas, marriages, deaths, births, illness, but I've always managed to cope with whatever life throws at me. I had a successful career in sales and marketing, travelled the world with my job, and have two wonderful healthy children. I chose to remove alcohol from my life 24 years ago, I didn't want to become dependent, so it was an internal conscious decision.

"I set up and had my own successful construction company for the last 20 years and navigated my way through. That was up until four years ago when I allowed another person to completely destroy me. That's when I was diagnosed with PTSD, but I pulled through that with time and self-help."

"This current situation that I find myself in, well, it started ten months ago, maybe longer, or maybe it's all intertwined."

Another Psychiatrist made an attempt to interrupt me; I sat calm and allowed it to happen.

"You've had Suicidal thoughts and ideology?"

"I have, yes, within the last several months, I am not proud of myself, allowing these thoughts to take me over. I've acted out the process hundreds of times in my mind, and I also made a noose for myself and tested it out many times, but clearly never carried it out. I still have thoughts, but they're more based on feelings of hopelessness. I've also considered committing a crime serious enough to get me locked up, a bank robbery, and time in prison. I know it's fantasy, but I just want to escape from what I'm going through, but I know these actions are not the answer."

It was at this point, for the first time in months, I really wanted to talk about what I believed I was going through, right there, right now. I hadn't mentioned to anyone in my family or friends what I truly knew was going on within me.

Holding my hands up to signal time out, the room fell coldly silent. I scanned the panel of specialists arranged in front of me,

With Tim directly ahead of me, I checked in with each one of them, non-verbally, just eye contact and held my gaze for several seconds with each one. Within me, there was something I had to explain in my words. Nothing related to my history other than what I had started to experience within the last twelve, fifteen months.

I had nothing to lose, and for the first time in months, fear had left my body and mind. This was my opportunity to convey, without judgment, to a bunch of strangers what I knew was happening to me.

"I am going through what I understand to be a spiritual awakening, a full-blown awakening. I understood it to begin with what I was experiencing. It bears no resemblance to anything that's gone before me; it made sense, you see, 12 months ago. I realized a lifelong dream to write a book, a true story that involved my family, and with the assistance of a good friend, that dream became a reality.

The process was life-changing, and for months I was living in a state of bliss; everything was working well; my business was operating and making good money; I'd even recovered from a serious car accident which has gravely damaged my back.

I was learning new things, reading again, researching, planning for changes, and even enrolling in a course to become a practitioner in Hypnotherapy and life coaching."

"Then, some small things changed in my life; the coping strategies I had previously relied on and that had served me well appeared to have deserted me.

I was struck with fear, something I had never suffered with, suddenly, I was back to using a walking stick. In my work, I was using excuses, not getting things finished, and becoming unreliable. My self-doubt became the main thought process; yes, I was spiralling into a dark hole.

Whatever I did to alleviate it, somehow it plunged me further into where I found myself with the noose and now sitting here in a secure unit.

In the shortest of times, I have relinquished and lost my former self and everything associated with my life. I have entered into bankruptcy, my business is gone, my income, my self-respect, I have lost family and friends, and I believe I am living through my dark night of the soul, but I will come through it, somehow, with faith, belief and resilience,

I will rise again. I know I am not insane; I also know I am not a danger to myself or anyone else. This moment, right here, now, sat in front of you all, this is my rock bottom, but I have within me, I know within me is the strength to rebuild."

It was the bright light from the security guards torch, out of nowhere, now stood directly in front of me, raising my left hand to shield the glare, " I know," I said calmly, "I'm leaving now, no problem, just been gathering my thoughts."

He wasn't in the mood for polite conversation, and I had done enough talking for one day. As I walked up the tree-lined avenue of the main hospital grounds, he walked two metres behind me. Inside I raised a laugh and a brief smile; ironic, I arrived last night under police supervision, and now 26 hours later, I was being escorted off the facility,

Where was I walking to? There was only one place to go; I had to take the next right step and walk into the next chapter.

Joseph Loney

As this is written, Joseph Loney is 55 years of age, a single man with two beautiful adult children who are living their best lives.

Who is he? He has a vivid memory of first asking himself that question at eight years old; born to Irish parents and one of four, he was third into the sibling hierarchy, raised in a traditional Irish Catholic family. He questioned everything but mostly was unheard, so he made up his own mind and did his own thing. Forty-two years after first asking himself the question, *"Who am I, "* and *"What is my reason for existing*?"* at age 50, those questions would hit him like a truck travelling towards him at high speed, and he was pushed and shunted off the cliff edge.

A Spiritual Awakening, really? You're an Empath, Joseph, really? He had to Google that! Being told he was the strongest, the most resilient person others knew meant nothing to him.

The wonderful life he had lived, all the amazing and beautiful memories, children, houses, cars, boats, a successful business life, marriages, deaths, a best-selling published book, within the shortest of times, it all meant nothing to him.

He is living proof and history that reaching into the darkest of places, believing there was no way out, standing on the edge of life and death; what stopped him from taking his own life ?

Something deep within him? He had to dig so deep it was a huge excavation of inner work.There is a way; it takes strength and resilience, it is within, and it needs locating and unlocking; how is it done? Well, that's what he wants to tell you, in his own words, his own life experiences, what he learned, what he found out and what he is doing now. We are all works in progress; we are what we think.

He allows this moment to be as it is!

THE LADDER OF SUCCESS

Amanda M Renaud

The world of business is forever changing and growing, and people all over the world are seeking new, unique and innovative ideas to change and compete in the world of business.

With many motivated entrepreneurs seizing the markets and continually fighting to compete across all industries, becoming successful can be the result of thoughts lingering in our rearview mirrors that turn into dreams. If you are not quick enough to take action and have the courage to take risks, someone else may beat you to it.

One of the keys to achieving success is understanding some key fundamentals in moving up the ladder of success. The first step I refer to as the spark; the drive to climb. For many, it is making a commitment and dedicating yourself to achieving a goal with a purpose and plan. It takes one spark or idea to begin your journey.

With everything in the world moving fast and being in a very competitive society, as entrepreneurs, we always have to ensure we are creative, always working, assessing, planning, and putting our knowledge into action. You are more likely to accomplish something if you are committed and take action immediately. Procrastination will not ensure you move up the ladder of success. If you can dream it, you can do it. It's really a matter of how badly you want something and how committed you are.

There will be many around you who won't understand your vision or will think you are crazy because of your ideas, but do not let others who are full of fear direct your journey. The next phase is assessment and understanding where you are progress-wise. How are you tracking your progress? How do you know you are doing what needs to be done? Create a way to monitor your progress and be honest about where you are.

Another key fundamental is resilience. You have to be resilient and understand that not everything will go as planned. Plan and be prepared for things to go sideways. Ensure you always have a backup plan.

Your integrity will be one thing you will need to be mindful of while achieving any goal. A lot of people who strive for success become ego-driven rather than passion-driven, and that really is trouble. You have to be able to maintain those professional relationships while networking.

True character always becomes exposed when you start to become successful, and you think you don't need others, but everyone around you has a purpose. Those around you are potential consumers of products or services you have to offer. It is the shared knowledge, opportunities, and potential for growth that lead to success. Always remain humble and take breaks if you start to get some resistance or start getting overwhelmed.

When others see you do your best, some will become jealous or envious, and that's normal. Some will tell you no, some will judge or mock you, but all of that is irrelevant, and it should be viewed as fuel and motivation. None of those actions by others or that type of treatment feels good. Of course, you have to be able to push past any skepticism or criticism and keep going. People always think you're outlandish when it comes to new ideas or different life paths, but be true to what you want and who you are.

Be resourceful and solution-focused, and remain adamant in your choices. View every challenge as a milestone, like an equation that needs solving, rather than just an impending incident of doom. There is always a way to make life work for you and accomplish all that you are passionate about. Some may not see the value in what you have to offer or what you can do, and that is fairly common. Find others who do see the value.

Most people in society don't see the big picture or what you are trying to accomplish, and that's also normal. That is why you have to do the impossible and offer something no one else can. You will always find a way if you are dedicated to your journey. All that you go through in life is not for nothing.

I am a believer that all the hardships and struggles we face are to teach us, shape us, and prepare us. When we experience good and bad, it changes how our brain views the world. We become warriors of success rather than just slaves to our own minds, which can sometimes be oppressive.

In order to be successful, you are going to have to keep climbing and never be afraid to reach the top, embrace every step, and not fear what's ahead. Some will give up on their dreams early in life because they get tired. It's crucial to keep healthy mindsets and things you are passionate about in your life to keep you energized. I believe anyone can do anything they want in life. If you want something bad enough, you will make it happen.

I also tell others that failure is okay, too. It's normal. Failure is one of life's biggest teachers, alongside self-reflection. You do not wake up and hit a home run, you wake up, and you practice and master your skill, then you hit that home run. Failure is not a declaration of character; it is a key element in the foundation of success. If you can look at what went wrong critically and draft ways to make it work better next time, that is an honourable act of growth. Failure is a fundamental part of assessment and planning for ascending the ladder of success.

As we begin to weed out the behaviours, actions, and attitudes that no longer serve us or help us become successful, we find things getting easier. We must always be willing to adjust our plans and make changes to reach our full potential and move up the ladder of success. When failure is viewed from this aspect, it is not really a failure. It becomes a teachable moment rather than a negative event.

The first step up the ladder of success is always going to be the spark. That's the vision, the idea, and the overall goal of what you want to achieve. The second step is to start planning how you will get there and make an action plan and a timeline for what you want to accomplish by a certain date.

Plan for bumps in the road because there will always be some. Honour and celebrate where you are in your journey of progression, and reflect on it regularly. Eliminate distractions and derailment, and stay committed to your timeline. If you miss goal markers, that's alright. However, do not make it a habitual practice.

In order to achieve success, you have to include rituals, habits, and routines. It takes an element of self-discipline and self-care. Both are crucial in achieving the highest level of accomplishment. It's a mutual understanding between yourself and the world around you that in order to do your best, you must feel your best.

One of the things I often explain to people around me is that it's necessary to understand self-care and how important it is. My life is exceptionally busy with three children and assisting other family members in our home on a day-to-day basis. I had to set a strict routine for myself and stay dedicated to it.

I set the alarm for 3:30 a.m. every day and took that time to do my writing, get everyone ready for their day, and then go to work for 10-12 hours a day. It was exhausting and eventually led to burnout when life stressors began to pile up. It was challenging to navigate through some life-changing events, but I stayed committed and eventually accomplished everything I wanted to. When dreams start getting further behind schedule, it's a good sign to reassess what you are doing and get a handle on that quickly.

Another factor is that you can not surround yourself with people who do not take life seriously and expect to thrive. Your environment also contributes to a lot of what you can achieve. As entrepreneurs, we have to be surrounded by like-minded people who are passionate about learning and growing. If you are sacrificing who you are to fit in, the cost is too high. When people do not believe in you, it shows. When they don't value you, it shows. Those people are not likely going to change their stance. So change where you stand. So I say to others, "Go where there is love and support and flourish like your life depends on it. Because it does." If you want to do great things, then surround yourself with others who have the same vision as you. Do not invest your time and dedication in dead zones. Dead zones are areas of life or environments that you can not go any further or that do not allow you to grow or provide opportunity for you to learn and fuel your growth.

The problem many entrepreneurs face today is that most of us have a hunger for growth, learning, and success, and when you are around places and people who do not, it makes it extremely hard to keep your flame burning. Toxic environments and toxic people are more likely to change you long before you change them if you do not know how to navigate them properly with skill.

In order to keep climbing the ladder of success, you must have a level of understanding of what is happening around you at all times and take a solution-based approach and have a sense of creativity to make impacts that last and help you reach the top. Everything matters, and every interaction and connection you make is vital. A lot of people typically do not see the value in others and the smaller steps needed to get to the stop. Every single milestone and step matters. Life should always be working for you and not the other way around.

Success is always difficult, and what it looks like for each person will vary. The most important thing in order to keep climbing is your drive. Fuel that drives you to keep going, and if what you're doing is not contributing to your overall success, stop doing it. Find a different way to get there. Success requires you to step outside your comfort zone and embrace risk. A lot of individuals become intimidated or overwhelmed by new challenges or bumps in the road. The way to combat those inner thoughts is to change the way you think about the situation and view the world around you by including more positive thoughts in your assessments.

Some use gratitude dairies or positive mantras. It's a matter of retraining your brain and everyday language to be more adamantine-focused. Your daily habits and the way you carry yourself will determine how fast you move up the ladder of success. We all have insecurities and thoughts that are not helpful, but we have to learn how to silence them and replace those behaviours and habits in ways that complement where we want to go.

The world can be cold and cruel, but if we are not eliminating barriers and controlling the elements that no longer serve us, we can be sucked into a spiral of unhelpful thinking patterns. Our thoughts contribute to our behaviours and what we accomplish. When we are not focused, inspired, or motivated, it's not likely we will meet our goals. The better we become and the healthier our minds and habits are, the faster we can achieve our goals to attain success.

To truly become successful individuals, we must invest in ourselves and work through all the things that cause us inward distress. Once you realize you can not control everything around you, and all you can control is yourself and your own response, you become a powerful individual capable of achieving anything.

Most people base success on financial status and social status. The truth is that success is truly a measurement of happiness, health, and accomplishment. Money is a helpful tool but not a definitive measurement. Wealth and glamour are often depicted as success, but it's not the truth. If you can achieve all you want and do it with integrity and honesty, that is true success. If you can bring something to the table that no one else can and be confident in that, you can avoid mindsets like the imposter syndrome.

Many entrepreneurs can suffer from imposter syndrome, and mostly, it stems from lack of confidence, unhealed trauma, and a lack of boundaries. When we believe in ourselves, set those boundaries, heal, and accept failures as a part of the learning curve of the ladder of success, we can truly make progress and disarm any mindsets and behaviours that do not help us climb that ladder.

Being self-aware and making a commitment to reflect, plan, and navigate through uneasy moments, provides the right footing to move up that ladder. Some of the negative commonalities I have seen in my experience of being a leader are the unwillingness of others to want to learn, listen to mentors and leaders, the lack of conflict resolution, not being able to let go of things that do not work or are not helpful, lack of navigating changes and goal setting and lastly lack of motivation.

These commonalities can cause a riptide of unhelpful behaviours and thinking patterns that do not serve others in a way that allows them to be open to accomplishment and meeting targets. If, as entrepreneurs, we do not act quickly on recourse, it can decimate an environment and can really impact everyone in a toxic way.

If entrepreneurs are not aware of these barriers, it's likely we may fall into the trap of complacency, and it will change us and prevent us from becoming successful long before we change it. Success and opportunity come to those who are self-aware and truly want to make an everlasting impact on themselves and the people around them.

Do not ever underestimate the power and presence one person like yourself can have in any setting. You can achieve anything you desire. It comes down to how badly you want it and much dedication you are willing to put forth in order to climb that ladder.

Amanda M Renaud

Amanda is a 36-year-old woman with three sons, who was born in Toronto, Ontario, but currently resides in the small town of Waubaushene, Ontario. Amanda is a car accident survivor and suffers from a traumatic brain injury, but that has never stopped her from succeeding or helping others around her.

Amanda completed over seven years of rehabilitation therapy and never let her physical struggles or traumas stop her from accomplishing her goals. She has many years of leadership experience and has had a very unique walk of life.

Although she has had many struggles in her life, she has worked very hard to become an inspirational leader everywhere she goes. Amanda holds a degree in Child and Youth Treatment and is striving every day to become a well-recognized author across the globe in hopes of helping others and sharing her remarkable stories of survival, and teaching others how to be true leaders and live a better life.

Amanda, despite her struggles, is a highly motivated individual with a passion for reading and writing and is always eager to teach others how to succeed. She was a featured co-author in the *Magnetic Entrepreneur for Women in Leadership* book in 2019 and is eager to pursue her career as an inspiring author.

Amanda is the true definition of resilience; she has faced adversity and has demonstrated a vast knowledge of self-development. She hopes to one day change the world with her

knowledge and writing. She is a bright young lady with a sense of humour and plans one day to own a publishing company and help others get their message out to the world.

WHY LEADERS NEED TO GIVE BACK TO THEIR COMMUNITY

Natalie L. Boehm

When we see the image of leaders in the media, we normally picture people with fancy cars, private jets, and huge mansions. While success does open up those opportunities to some leaders, the euphoria that they bring is short-lived. Sure, it looks great when you can show off a private jet, but what does that say about you? Do you need material items to feel complete - to feel successful, or are there other ways you can feel complete and make the euphoric feeling last long-term?

As you grow as a leader, it is important to give back to the community. It is important to understand how to contribute and to understand the different ways that people and businesses contribute.

There are three ways people and companies contribute; charity, philanthropy, and corporate social responsibility. **Charity is defined as generosity and helpfulness**, especially toward the needy or suffering (Merriam-Webster, n.d.). Charity is often linked to a one-time donation. Examples would be taking clothing down to a homeless shelter or giving a one-time financial donation to a local charity.

Philanthropy is defined as an active effort to promote human welfare (Merriam-Webster, n.d.). Examples of philanthropy would be giving a monthly donation or volunteering on a regular basis to an organization or multiple organizations. When people hear the word philanthropy, the first thing they picture is someone like Bill Gates. You don't have to be a billionaire to contribute to your community. You can contribute to organizations in your community that have a mission you support without breaking the bank.

You can be a philanthropist as a leader, or if you are a CEO, you can do philanthropy through your company. The important thing is to become a philanthropist for the right reason. Many will do it feeling it is a great way to build their brand. While building your brand is important, it is more important to invest in your community and make a positive impact on those who are less fortunate.

Corporate social responsibility is defined as a self-regulating business model that helps a company be socially accountable to itself, its shareholders, and the public (Fernando, 2022). Corporate social responsibility has had many mixed reviews. Many feel that multinational organizations need to help make a commitment to our world.

People against corporate social responsibility feel that businesses are there to work in creating profits and honouring their stakeholders and that government and nonprofit organizations are to focus more on poverty, social justice, and serving underserved communities. According to the article, *12 Socially Responsible Companies to Applaud,* ninety percent of consumers are likely to trust and be loyal to socially responsible companies compared to those that are not.

Companies can take part in corporate social responsibility that does have a positive impact on their shareholders, the public and can strengthen their brand. Mastercard has set a positive example in implementing diversity, equity, and inclusion into their company's operations and in the community. As companies grow, it is important to create career opportunities for communities that have faced economic challenges, such as African Americans, the LGBTQIA+ community, people with disabilities and differences, and many more.

Many professionals who fall into these categories face stigma, resulting in them fighting for career, economic, and educational opportunities that others take for granted. In 2021, Mastercard focused on pay equity, announcing that women, African Americans, Hispanic, and Asian employees earn one dollar for every dollar that is earned by white employees, including base, bonuses, and long-term incentives (Mastercard, 2021). By implementing these changes into their company, not only does it show that Mastercard is willing to make changes to have a more positive impact on their company and strengthen their brand, but these decisions have a positive impact on society, helping to employ people who may not have had the opportunity.

Mandating equal pay is viewed in a positive way that communities that are under DEI (Diversity, Equity, Inclusion) will look into working for a company like Mastercard. It is companies like this that individuals, especially the younger generation, are looking to invest in. It creates a win-win situation for society and for Mastercard.

This is an excellent example of corporate social responsibility and strengthens the argument that corporations, especially multinational companies, should be working to grow their companies, create a strong return on investment for their shareholders, but also create actions within their company that have a positive impact on the company and society.

No matter what level you are at as a leader, whether it be a small business or large corporation, giving back is not just important but has many benefits. In the article, *The Importance of Giving Back,* the author lists four important benefits that leaders and companies gain when they give back:

1.   Network Expansion

Many organizations involved in philanthropy have board members who are business leaders. Being involved in philanthropic organizations not only looks good on the board leaders, but businesses can point to them and show they have a team member who is contributing to society. It creates the opportunity to make more connections and create possible collaboration opportunities.

2.   Empowering Employees

Leaders can bring their team members together to help fundraise or volunteer for a charitable cause, showing not just teamwork but that they have established a healthy climate and can unite everyone. Working together and helping an important cause can bring a team together and demonstrate to the community and company that together, they can accomplish goals and are unified.

3.   Business Reputation

Reputation can make or break an organization, no matter the size. Businesses rely on keeping a strong reputation established, especially small business owners. If a multinational company does something that is not good, short-term, it looks bad, but long-term, they have the connections to recover. The average small business owner does not have those connections. Keeping customers happy is important. What makes them even happier, besides providing a great product or service, is seeing you involved in the local community, helping to make an impact. Funding a local project, donating supplies to a local school district, or helping a food bank feed local families is a great way to build a reputation, establish yourself as an important contributor to the community, and gain more customers.

4.   Good Marketing

In the article, the author mentioned a 2015 study conducted by Cone Communications based on corporate social responsibility and millennials. The study stated that "more than 9-in-10 millennials would switch brands to one associated with a cause (Cone Communications, 2015). This is true, and it has pressured companies, especially newer companies, to show they can be sustainable and help others. TomboyX, a company that makes activewear, sports bras, and more, established their company just that way, helping them to go from a small startup in Seattle to a B corporation that has done great things within their company and society.

TomboyX creates products that are gender neutral, offering a wide range in sizes, creates clothing to help reduce gender dysphoria, and works towards empowering the LGBTQIA+ community. What started as a goal by founders Fran Dunaway and Naomi Gonzales to create the perfect gender-neutral boxer brief turned into a corporation providing products to many in a community who feel the fashion industry has underrepresented them.

One thing that the author did not mention is the impact it has on you as a human being. Sure, it looks good if you contribute to those less fortunate, but did you know there are health benefits to giving? According to Cleveland Clinic, giving to others releases positive neurotransmitters such as serotonin, dopamine, and oxytocin, all helping to regulate mood, giving you a sense of pleasure, and creates connections with others. Not just that, but giving can help to lower blood pressure, increase your lifespan, and reduce stress. I think all of us can agree that we all would enjoy having a little less stress in our lives.

The reason I am passionate about giving as a leader comes down to one thing; as humans, I feel it is the right thing to do; you don't know when you will be the one in need. For years I have been involved in giving to charity, many different ones over the years. I have been a guardian for the Erie County Animal Shelter, where I adopted my cats, I sponsored a child in Sierra Leone for five years, I have given to many organizations for advocacy on a humanitarian basis. In 2020, I created my nonprofit organization to give back to the epilepsy community, which with I was diagnosed in 1980. I made up my mind not to allow having a neurological condition stop me from living life, and I am advocating to help others gain the strength to do the same. There are many ways, as a leader, you can be involved in giving and making a positive impact for your community. If you haven't yet, take the first step now and start. For those of you already making a difference, great job; keep it up and help create change. We all need to do our part.

Resources:

Cleveland Clinic (2022). Why Giving Is Good for Your Health. *Cleveland Clinic Health Essentials.* Retrieved from:

https://health.clevelandclinic.org/why-giving-is-good-for-your-health/

Cone Communications (2015). New Cone Communications Research Confirms Millennials as America's Most Ardent CSR Supporters, but Marked Differences Revealed Among This Diverse Generation. *Cone Communications.* Retrieved from:

https://conecomm.squarespace.com/2015-cone-communications-millennial-csr-study-pdf/

Cantin, D. (2022). The Importance of Giving Back. *Forbes Business Council.* Retrieved from:

https://www.forbes.com/sites/forbesbusinesscouncil/2022/05/31/the-importance-of-giving-back/?sh=707e87b47139

Fernando, J. (2022). Corporate Social Responsibility (CSR) Explained With Examples. *Investopedia.* Retrieved from: https://www.investopedia.com/terms/c/corp-social-responsibility.asp

Mastercard (2021). Diversity, Equity, Inclusion: Creating limitless possibilities for everyone. *Mastercard.* Retrieved from: https://www.mastercard.us/en-us/vision/who-we-are/diversity-inclusion.html

Merriam-Webster. (n.d.). Charity. In Merriam-Webster.com dictionary. Retrieved January 6, 2023, from https://www.merriam-webster.com/dictionary/charity

Merriam-Webster. (n.d.). Philanthropy. In the Merriam-Webster.com dictionary. Retrieved January 6, 2023, from https://www.merriam-webster.com/dictionary/philanthropy

Morgan, M. (2022). LGBTQ+, Gender-Inclusive Underwear Brand, TomboyX Announces B Corp Certification. *Cision PR Newswire*. Retrieved from: https://www.prnewswire.com/news-releases/lgbtq-gender-inclusive-underwear-brand-tomboyx-announces-b-corp-certification-301508237.html

Natalie Boehm

Natalie Boehm is an author, disability activist, and strategic consultant. She is the author of *The Formula for Success* and the president of *The Defeating Epilepsy Foundation*. Natalie's passion is to educate others and help them achieve the goals they desire, despite any challenges they may face. Natalie obtained her master's in business administration from the University of Redlands and has completed certifications in organizational management, leadership development, and nonprofit management. She resides in California with her husband and sons.

Transformation IS Possible

Ivy Perez

"We need to realize that our path to transformation is through our mistakes. We're meant to make mistakes, recognize them, and move on to become unlimited." - Yehuda Berg

Bad things happen to us all, wouldn't you agree? It doesn't matter if you're a good person or a bad person; no one is immune to something negative or tragic happening in their life at some point. For some, hardships start at a very early age and continue into adulthood.

For others, it can be a season in time. Understand that we are supposed to get through it and become stronger because of it. This happens not by white-knuckling it but by knowing that what's inside of you is far greater than any situation, circumstance, or challenge you are going through.

How we go through any situation determines our outcome. Our way of thinking and the mental tools we have in our toolbox will help us stand firm in the midst of chaos and move forward with more ease and grace.

A little backstory

I don't have much of a recollection with my father, maybe three occasions - him buying me a bike, a family lake outing, and him brushing my hair, but I do remember vividly the night when it would be the last time I would see him for years. I am the oldest of three girls, but for approximately three years, it was just me. I was Daddy's little girl. I always felt like number one.

As a child, approximately seven years old, I felt like I shut down emotionally toward my mom. I was angry with her for "throwing him out" and angry with my father, who "left me." Later I would experience sexual abuse and molestation.

At around ten years of age, alcohol crossed my path at a New Year's Eve party. In sixth grade, alcohol crossed my path again at a friend's house. It wouldn't be until my first year in college that I "learned" to drink heavily. Unfortunately, I thought that that way of drinking was normal, and I continued that way of drinking well into adulthood.

Adulthood

From my twenties into my forties, I was a mess on the inside. I was confused with life. I was angry with men. On the outside, I looked like I had it together because I learned how to cover up and mask how I felt. I moved every few years all throughout my childhood and every few years in my adulthood. I worked blindly. I moved across the country. I was constantly on the go.

Drinking progressively got worse in my thirties, and it would lead to a car accident, jail, losing my license, and a significant loss of income. A part of me felt like wherever I went, a dark cloud was hovering over me until I realized it was 'I' who was my own dark cloud.

I realized that wherever I went, there I was. I needed to work on myself. I needed to figure out why I was doing what I was doing. I was scared at this point in my life, but I was ready for change.

Transformation is a journey

"Transformation isn't sweet and bright. It's a dark and murky, painful pushing. An unraveling of the untruths you've carried in your body. A practice in facing your own created demons. A complete uprooting before becoming." - Victoria Erickson (Author, *Edge of Wonder*)

The beginning of my journey began when I was completely broken and shattered. I was drinking heavily and putting myself in dangerous situations. Sometimes I didn't care, but many times, I just wasn't thinking.

I would always say I had angels around me because, after a night of debauchery, I didn't have a clue as to how I got home, where I parked, or even remembered the events of the evening. I would follow that statement up, however, with, "But, one of these days, the angels are not going to be there." I would say this because I knew in my heart that it was I that needed to learn my lesson and grow.

That day did come. I rear-ended a vehicle one evening that caused me to get arrested, booked for a DUI and processed, which was THE MOST humiliating and traumatic event in my life.

After that experience, I was quite frankly ready to dig deep. This was a huge wake-up call for me to begin the process of finding out who I was.

Soon thereafter, my eyes were opened to quantum physics. I was flabbergasted and yet very intrigued. I grew up Catholic, and because of my childhood "stuff," I pushed God away. This information, this science, made so much sense to me, even though I didn't fully understand it. It was as if the pieces of a 1000-piece puzzle box of my life were starting to come together.

The thing is, I never had direction. I never had someone in my life, whether a parent, family member, friend, colleague, or boss, that would help me with my thinking until that juncture. I was determined to figure myself out in order to change my life.

I wouldn't truly start this process of conscious learning and having more "awareness" until I was about 45. Better late than never, right?

Hindsight is 20/20

In 2017, I was let go from a job for the first time in my life. Four days later, however, I was at a three-day immersive DreamBuilder event. By the second day, I resonated with everything the company was about - their mission and purpose. When their coaching program was presented, it was an easy 'yes.' Although an "easy" yes, there was the immediate rise of fear and ALL the thoughts of why I shouldn't and couldn't flooded my mind.

I knew I had to take the leap. I knew that I had to listen to the part of me that wanted to win for the first time in my life, rather than the part of me that wanted to continue playing small.

So I signed up and went through a rigorous training program. I became a certified transformational life coach. I now get the honour to couple my life experiences with codified principles to help others transform their lives in any endeavour that is meaningful to them.

I ask you, is there anywhere in your life where you are playing small? Is there an area in your life where you are unhappy? Perhaps you're "dealing with" a job for a paycheque? Maybe even worse, every single day, you walk through the doors at your job, and you feel the life force energy sucked right out of you. Are you in a relationship that is toxic? Did you let yourself go, and you're dealing with health issues because of it?

When you really think about it, you know exactly what that thing is, that is a major dissatisfaction in your life. Not a good place to be, I know, but I promise you, you don't have to live that way.

BECOMING

We all have a dream inside of us somewhere, even if we are endeavouring to find it, or we are in the process of achieving it.

I invite you to ask this question, "What would I love?" This is a highly calibrated question and one that I ask of my clients all the time and even of myself when I don't feel aligned in a certain area in my life. Think of the four main life domains - Health and Wellness, Relationships, Vocation or Avocation, and Time & Money Freedom.

I had two dreams that I thought were not possible for me. One was to let go of alcohol's grip on my life. The other was to become a triathlete.

My "Free From Alcohol" DREAM

The desire to be alcohol-free came about in my late 30s, as I mentioned, when I was shattered and broken. I knew for a long time I would be better off without it; I just didn't have the tools to help me mentally and spiritually make it happen. From my training, I gained those tools and more. My sobriety date is June 1, 2018. I was 48.

My Triathlon DREAM

My triathlon dream was written down and verbalized for the first time in my life at the DreamBuilder event. We had gone through a powerful "dream building" exercise. It would be three years after this that I registered for, trained for, and achieved my first triathlon. I was one month shy of my 53rd birthday.

YOUR Dream

I know you have a dream inside of you, and if you don't know what that is right now, that's okay. There is a process that will help you to uncover and discover your dream like the proverbial "magic wand." We are here on this Earth as human beings in physical form, but we are incredible spiritual beings with amazing gifts inside of us.

LIVE LIFE FULLY NOW

"Develop your imagination – you can use it to create in your mind what you hope to create in your life." Stephen Covey

We have been conditioned to look outside of ourselves for answers when the answers are already within. Our Creator has gifted us with six mental faculties - imagination, intuition, memory, reason, will and perception - but we are taught to lean on our five senses.

By understanding our mental faculties, we are able to tap into their power. We can then step into creating a life and environment we want for ourselves. When we recognize our gifts and understand that life will challenge us, we can consciously and spiritually know that we will get through it because there is a lesson to be learned.

I now guide, encourage, and support women and men, helping them understand who they came to be in this life; to recognize that their past does not dictate their future, to notice that when you focus on looking in the rearview mirror of your life, you muddle your present and distort your future.

My passion is helping you see possibilities for your life and believe in the power within you, to take the small necessary steps forward, to not just design a dream for your life, but to step into the belief and the deserving of it.

My passion, too, is to help you rise above limiting beliefs and limiting expectations and circumstances.

If by reading this, you feel a nudge or a whisper, pay attention. That is your inner guide wanting you to explore possibilities for your life. Perhaps it is a calling. Only you know what that thing is that you desire or long for. Remember that God or the Universe will send you two signals for growth. Those two signals are your longing and discontent. The question is, will you listen to that part of you that wants to play bigger in your life?

I paid attention to the longing at the Dreambuilder event. The decision wasn't easy, nor was it convenient. Remember, I had lost my job just four days prior. There was no money coming in, and it was the largest investment I had ever made, but the pull was so strong that I had to say yes. I said yes to wanting something bigger for my life and my family's life.

Isn't now your time?

Ivy Perez

Ivy Perez is a proud mom, marathoner, triathlete, breast cancer survivor and has been sober from alcohol since 2018. Extremely passionate about mindset, self-improvement and personal empowerment, she's earned two degrees - BA in Biology/Environmental Science & a BS in Information Technology. However, it was her rigorous training to become certified in transformational life coaching that was/is the most life-changing for her, and now, she gets to guide, support and encourage women who are at a crossroads in their life.

She loves to help women find their spark, feel good about themselves again, uncover and discover their purpose, design a dream, and implement simple mindset tools to create a fuller, more expansive life NOW.

Ivy has also spoken on many stages, whether it be on virtual summits, podcasts or at live events. Her passion and expertise in mindset and movement moves people to start making changes in their lives. It is her mission to get people to BE and DO healthier.

Ivy is also a co-author in three books: *Spiritual Fitness Survivor Series - How to Turn Your Struggles Into Strength, 2nd edition*, *Self empowerment Reset Series - Our Conversations with the Divine* and *Collaborate to Succeed - Partnering with Top Entrepreneurs for Business Growth*.

Taking the first step can sometimes be the scariest, but it does not have to be. Allow her the honour to guide and cheer you on your journey to fulfillment.

To connect with Ivy,: https://linktr.ee/ivy_perez or email at: DreamBuildwithIvy@gmail.com

AGAINST ALL ODDS: A JOURNEY TO SUCCESS

Juanita Kapp

My name is Juanita Kapp, and I am proud to be who I am today.

I was rejected at birth by my father, who didn't want a daughter but a son. In those days, doctors couldn't discern the gender of the baby before the actual birth occurred. He made my mother buy everything in blue. He was a very abusive man who had, during the years of their marriage, become an alcoholic. Don't misunderstand me. He was a brilliant helicopter pilot who excelled in everything he did. He had the opportunity to qualify for his career in the US and came back to build his family and work on my grandfather's game farms.

On the day of my birth, he simply looked at my mother and said, "Real men have sons." Then he walked away and didn't return to the hospital. The abuse at home continued and slowly but surely got worse. He never held me until I was one year old. That day, I was sick and crying profusely, which angered him. He took me and threw me against the wall to silence me. My mom finally realized that it was time to change our circumstances and left him. I don't remember what he looks like, and I have never heard from him since.

Sadly, my Mom passed away in 2020 from Stage 4 brain cancer. She was only 65 years old. I have since come to realize through my years of study that she never had an opportunity to get rid of the trauma that she had faced when I was small. He used to hang her by her hair in the shed while she was pregnant with me and did other horrible things as well. I will explain that in detail when I write my book later in 2023.

Why do I start writing this chapter on such a traumatic note? I do so on purpose because I want to highlight the fact that although we are sometimes brought into this world in negative circumstances, it doesn't determine our future. It also isn't a precursor for the God-given potential that lies embedded deep within us.

I was teased in school for not having a Dad. It made me believe that there was something wrong with me, that I wasn't good enough and that I lacked purpose. I was also teased because I had sweaty palms, which forced me to go to school with a washcloth every day as my schoolbooks would be drenched in sweat during class.

Then one day, I decided to address the underlying fear and anxiety which caused my palms to sweat excessively. I started to audibly tell myself that I wasn't afraid of anything or anyone and that I didn't need to worry. My palms stopped sweating, and I was finally able to attend school like a normal student by the time I was in high school.

I was born with one leg that was shorter than the other. The doctor mentioned that it could have been an injury that was overlooked as a child. Either that or it was a birth defect. That didn't stop me from excelling in sports, it only meant that I had to work harder than the other athletes. I was an excellent student in school. I thrived in academics, sports, extracurricular and all other areas of development. I won awards and trophies and always ended up in the top 10 academic students. I was on a mission, and I wasn't going to let anyone stop me.

I have come a long way since then, but it took a lot of courage and introspection to change the things about myself that I didn't like. I had to face reality and learn that my life is what I make of it. I had to understand that my destiny ultimately lies within my control.

It has been a journey of pain, anger, revelation and sadness. It also didn't happen overnight. Two failed marriages later, I found myself a single mother (just like my Mom). Both my marriages were to abusive men, one physical and one verbal/mental. After my second divorce, I realized that I had to work on self-love and inherent respect. I started to believe in myself again like I did when I was in high school and could see the difference it was making in my life.

I journeyed on like this for years and still had some toxic traits that needed to be dealt with. I had an anger problem, and I was a people pleaser. After having been hurt countless times by individuals that seemed to be my friends, I decided to start living for myself, not in a negative way but in an empowering fashion.

I started working on my discernment more and delved into my personal power. One thing I can say for sure is that I have always believed in treating everyone I meet with dignity and utmost respect. That is something about me that will never change.

In 2013 I was still serving as a full-time pastor but decided to start doing leadership training in the corporate world. I thoroughly enjoyed it and learned a lot. After a few months, I decided to move into the entrepreneurial space as well and started my business Meticulous.

At first, Meticulous only included public speaking services and video editing services. Through the years, it has grown in leaps and bounds. My role as a pastor equipped me greatly to become an effective and well-versed networker.

After my second divorce in 2020, I was removed by the Executive council from my pastoral position and stripped of my title. It didn't matter that I was stuck in an abusive marriage for 15 years. I was given an ultimatum: either stay in the marriage (which didn't progress in all those years) or be left out in the cold. I made it easy for them. I couldn't stomach the fact that they would rather have me live a fake life at home and then preach and minister on a Sunday as if nothing was going on behind the scenes. I will choose integrity every time.

In 2020, the onset of Covid-19 brought about many tower moments in my life. I call them the four "M's," and I will list them here below:

My Ministry started failing as all the churches were closed, and we couldn't work with the flock.

What was left of my Marriage finally fell apart.

I almost wasn't able to complete my Masters as I was a long-distance student, and I couldn't reach my invigilators. Thank God I was able to complete it.

My Mom passed away on July 5th, 2020, from stage 4 brain cancer.

Out of all of these events, my Mom's deteriorating condition was the most traumatic. I got the call shortly after that our entire country would be put under lockdown for exactly three weeks. My Mom phoned me crying and shared the news.

They had taken her to the hospital because all the doctor's offices were closed. She had a severe earache and thought she had a middle ear infection. It was something worse. She had cancer. It was aggressive, and she was at her last.

Because of the Covid-19 regulations, she wasn't able to take in a bag of clothes or her cell phone. She was there for three days before she was able to share the news with us. She was given three weeks to live. We were going to be under lockdown for three weeks. I wouldn't be able to reach her as I lived 900 kilometres away. I was broken.

The shock put me into an emotional spiral. For the first few days, I couldn't stop crying, and then one morning, I woke up and realized that I was powerful. I am powerful enough to change the particulars of my situation.

So, guess what I did? I started praying every day that she would live longer in order for me and my children to say our goodbyes. I sat on the corner of my bed in the sunlight every morning and looked at the mountains as I prayed Psalm 121:1

"I look unto the hills, where does my help come from? My help comes from the Lord Who has created the heavens and the earth." (paraphrased)

It worked! As the days went by, our lockdown was prolonged, and I kept praying and trusting. I used to phone her on WhatsApp (video calls), and we would talk about many things. We would laugh about childhood memories. We would cry together and talk about the things she still wanted to do in her life.

One morning I called her, and she couldn't hear what I was saying. She had lost her hearing, so we had to move over to texting and sending photos. By this time, she was far over the 3-week mark, and I was still battling to get a permit to be able to travel to her.

In the end, I reached her five days before she passed away. I held her hand that Sunday afternoon as she breathed her last breath. She had been in a coma since the day before. Suddenly she opened her eyes, looked at me and shed a tear. She closed them again, and then she was gone. She was too weak to squeeze my hand or to speak.

After conducting her funeral, I came back to fulfil my promise to her — that I would start to live with intention. The moment I arrived home, I hiked up my favourite mountain and sat there crying for hours. I slept for about three hours on my lion rock, too exhausted to journey down the mountain. Finally, when the sun began to set, I lifted myself up and walked down. On that day, my podcast *Meticulous Moments* was born.

Since then, I have focused extensively on my business and my personal growth. *Meticulous Moments* is all about facilitating Community Upliftment Through Leadership Development.

I now own various lucrative businesses and have expanded my horizons to another podcast, as well as other big projects. I am currently busy putting together three anthologies and have since moved into the publishing space.

Since 2022 I have been featured in three books, been a guest on over twenty podcasts, hosted four online conferences and won two awards (yet to be announced). I have been headhunted three times to work with executive teams globally. I am invited regularly to be a public speaker, MC, and teacher at events all over the world.

All the broken "M's" from 2020 has now been crafted into a beautiful and exotic "M" named "Meticulous" as I have finally found my purpose on earth. I am placed here in this timeline to be successful and to make the world a better place, one interview and one project at a time.

I love spreading joy and peace wherever I go. I love to inspire and ignite the hearts of everyone I meet. Because of all the brokenness that I have had to endure, the oil of anointing flows over my life, and I am able to raise the vibration wherever I go.

I will continue to be a strong and successful businesswoman. I have been training in martial arts since 2016 and have attained my 2nd Brown belt. Martial arts is a big part of my life. It has made me discover what I am capable of doing, and it has helped me to remove any and all fears out of my mind.

In business, we must be fearless. In business, we have to be great problem solvers, and these are the exact skills that Karate and MMA have taught me.

Listen to me closely. No rejection, no trauma, and no devastating event that transpires in your life can ever change your purpose.

Believe in yourself!

With love Juanita Kapp

Juanita Kapp

CEO at *Meticulous Moments*

Founder & Owner of the *Meticulous Moments Podcast*

Founder & Owner of the *Meticulous Martial Arts Mastermind*

Co-Founder & Owner of the *KAPPTOR Connection*

Co-Founder of the *Business Prowess* podcast

Executive team member at CLA

Executive team member at TPC

Executive team member at NBM

Hoinser Media Group Brand Ambassador

Since she was a young child, she has always wanted to "Tame the pen and the sword" and has made it her mission to do just that. She was an ordained Pastor for 15 years and enjoyed working with congregations. She always loved being a public speaker, author and Master of Ceremonies globally. In 2020 during the Covid-19 pandemic, Juanita decided to change her life and follow her heart's passion. She became an entrepreneur of note through pure willpower and personal choice.

She has since opened various businesses that are highly successful and has started to travel the world. Her newest venture is *Meticulous Safari's*, which she will be hosting in South Africa. She is excited about the future and the developments that it will present. Personal and Professional development have always been at the top of her priority list.

Travelling the globe and sharing her energy and positive outlook on life with those who cross her path has been a long-time goal. As an entrepreneur, she is a risk-taker. The sky is the limit in what we can achieve if only we would have the courage to believe.

A Rising Tide

Latara Dragoo

I was laid off on March 31 of 2020.

Without hesitating, I sprang into action. While most of the world froze in fear, I formed my S Corporation on April 20th, 2020.

It was a good thing I did!

My former boss shut the office down for several months.

When he finally re-started his business, he only took on a skeleton crew. They had to deal with the workload of the former staff, accompanied by the stress of trying to revive a failing business.

COVID had a multi-pronged attack strategy that walloped my former boss' business.

For one, the months of no income, the plethora of cancellations by customers, along with losing customers in droves played a huge part.

Then, because his business was a luxury real estate magazine publisher, there was the fact that during COVID, people pulled their listings off the market. In-person showings were virtually nonexistent, and homeowners were afraid of contact with the outside world, so for a long spell, there were almost no houses coming to the market.

Once properties did start flooding the market again, there was such a demand that realtors saw no need to advertise them in the magazine, or anywhere for that matter, as properties were flying off the shelves as soon as they were listed.

The last crippling blow happened months later, as COVID hit supply chains heavily; industries like printers, who had to pay through the nose to get their hands on paper supplies, passed along their price increases to their customers — publishers — one of those being my former boss.

So now he is seeing dwindling incoming ads being bought, and his overhead for running the show is now at least twice the cost, if not triple or beyond.

So you see, it was absolutely devastating for him and millions of business owners worldwide.

Restaurant owners went out of business. Brick-and-mortar businesses, even titans you would have never considered being weak, folded like a bad hand of cards.

Today, once-bustling shopping malls sit empty and sad.

Some restaurants are still take-out only. Going out to eat is not just about getting food; for that, there are grocery stores. It's all about the experience — and without the experience, it's hard to justify paying many times more for some groceries, even if they are ready to eat.

But I digress…

While the COVID shutdown was the final blow that crippled the company to such a debilitated state, it was not the whole story.

I could see that, while my former boss ran many "Print is Not Dead" campaigns, he refused to see the warning signs that, if print was not dead, it was at the very least shrinking, evolving, and falling out of favour.

I tried to warn him to take precautions and prepare for the oncoming blow by expanding his services. He was stubborn in doing anything other than what he knew — trying desperately to maintain the status quo. He was like a captain of a sinking ship trying to bail out the water with a leaky bucket.

I am sure my former boss wouldn't be too keen on the fact that I am sharing this info.

I did not talk about this for a long time. I felt like if the business I was doing marketing for, for 18 years, went under, then what does that say about my marketing abilities?

"Hire me so I can tank your business! Just look at my track record!"

But the fact of the matter is, my employment endured the Great Depression of 2008.

Before that, his publications saw their glory days. With 400-page thick issues and my boss hosting lavish events at $40-million estates, back then, he could afford to buy multiple houses, cars, and boats. His company was truly the epitome of luxury!

After the 2008 recession, his company limped along, had a couple of revitalizations, like when he branched out into open house newsletters, local tabloids, vacation rentals, and a Mega luxury magazine (only sporting properties that were $10 million and over). Instead of a solid vertical and core product, we expanded laterally, in order to save the company.

During that revitalization, I spearheaded the revamping of the company's website.

I thought it was going to really take off. But, despite the fact that my then-boss was 'gung-ho' about the website, it was almost as if he was missing the actual revenue-producing aspects of the site. It remained under-utilized for years. Then in retaliation, he removed all the bells and whistles that would entice customers to be long-term paying members. It was almost as if he wanted to punish potential advertisers for his own shortcomings out of frustration and spite.

Ultimately, to make a long story short, while COVID was a nasty adversary, his own stubbornness, fear, resentment, and inflexibility had led to his downfall.

I suppose my own response to being witness to this devastation in local businesses spurred me to move in the direction of helping business owners pivot into an online space.

I even created a local business website, an online directory that features locally owned businesses only in the San Diego area, called sandiegobuylocal.com.

But that was not enough. I realized that business owners who could pivot online thrived while their non-tech-savvy counterparts failed dismally.

These people should not be punished just because they are not an expert in tech. Their expertise is in their business. So that is why I became an online marketing strategist and IT consultant.

So now, I can step in to help these struggling business owners with the digital aspects of their business, so they can grow, scale, automate, flourish, and find their customers in the broader online market.

I truly believe that innovative thinking, along with flexibility, a pivot mindset, and quick, inspired action, can save small business owners from being taken down by the current paradigm shift.

For my top 3 tips on overcoming all obstacles by having a pivot mindset, watch this video: https://youtube/FwQfM2_R3bk

Latara Dragoo

Latara Dragoo is a Graphic Designer, Marketing Strategist and consultant who specializes in helping entrepreneurs, small business owners and coaches brand like a billion-dollar company.

With 18 years in the luxury publishing industry, 20 years of experience in marketing and graphic design, and ten years in online marketing, Latara is well-equipped to meet her clients' needs.

She dedicates her time to helping clients create a strong online presence and attract their ideal clients.

Her ultimate goal is to help busy, non-technical small business owners and coaches thrive in the new normal by providing outside-the-box, win/win solutions for their #1 problem in their business.

If you need help getting your vision out into the world, Latara is here to bring it to life and connect you to your target market in the digital world.

If you would like to get her free cheatsheet, ebook, and masterclass recording on how to create a strong online presence, connect, or find out more about her, please go to:

https://linktr.ee/latara.dragoo

FIGHTING FOOD INSECURITY
Chef Jagger Gordon

Chef Jagger Gordon has dedicated his life to philanthropy and fighting food insecurity globally. Growing up without food in his own fridge as a child, he experienced firsthand the challenges faced by many children in need. This inspired him to turn his life into a mission to help those who are struggling with food.

As a single father, Chef Jagger Gordon witnessed his daughter's friends also facing food insecurity. This motivated him to establish the *Feed It Forward* program.

Feed It Forward is a non-profit organization based in Toronto, Canada, that aims to fight food insecurity and reduce food waste. *Feed It Forward* operates various initiatives to address these issues and create a more sustainable and equitable food system while helping to eliminate food waste.

One of the notable projects of *Feed It Forward* is the Pay-What-You-Can Grocery Store and Restaurant. These unique concepts allow individuals and families facing food insecurity to access affordable and nutritious food, if not for free. Customers have the option to pay what they can afford or exchange volunteer hours for groceries or prepared food, ensuring that everyone has access to quality food regardless of their financial situation.

Feed it Forward rescues food from retail stores, manufacturers, distributors, and farmers and makes it available for customers at greatly reduced prices, (including free!). Individuals do not have to justify or explain their situation, allowing them the dignity to obtain nutritious food within their budget, whatever that is.

Feed It Forward also engages in rescue cooking, utilizing surplus and imperfect food that would otherwise go to waste. Chef Jagger Gordon and his team work closely with local farmers, grocery stores, and food suppliers to collect ingredients and transform them into nutritious meals that have already fed millions globally. These meals are then distributed to those in need through partnerships with shelters, community centers, the FeedItForward.ca Free food sharing App and other organizations.

In addition to their immediate impact on food security, *Feed It Forward* also raises awareness about food waste and its environmental and social consequences. By highlighting the importance of reducing food waste and promoting sustainable practices, they strive to create lasting change in the community.

The Feed It Forward App

One tool in advancing the *Feed It Forward* mission is *The Feed It Forward* free food app, designed to connect individuals and businesses with surplus food to those in need. It allows people who have food to donate to post it in their geographic region and people in need of food to see where food is available.

In this chapter, we explore Chef Jagger Gordon's visionary approach to make *Feed It Forward* accessible to people around the world by developing the app in different languages, including Ukrainian, Spanish and several more. We dive into the challenges and triumphs of expanding the app's reach, breaking down language barriers, and empowering individuals from diverse backgrounds to join the movement against food waste and hunger.

We delve into Chef Jagger Gordon's motivation to develop the *Feed It Forward* app recognizing the importance of reaching communities directly affected by food insecurity. We explore the cultural nuances and language considerations involved in creating multilingual platforms to ensure inclusivity and effective communication.

Here is an overview of how the application works:

• **User Registration:** Users can download the free Feed It Forward app from their respective app stores and create an account. They can register as either a food donor or a recipient.

• **Food Donors:** Businesses, restaurants, farmers, and individuals who have excess food can sign up as food donors. They provide details about the type of food, quantity, and location for pickup.

• **Food Listings:** Donors can list the available surplus food on the app, including a description, expiration date (if applicable), and any dietary restrictions or special instructions.

• **Notifications:** Once a food listing is posted, the app sends notifications to nearby recipients who match the food preferences and dietary needs specified in their profiles. Recipients can review the details and accept a donation if they are interested.

• **Pickup Coordination:** The app facilitates communication between the food donor and the recipient to coordinate the pickup logistics. They can discuss the time, location, and any additional instructions.

• **Food Collection:** The recipient collects the donated food directly from the donor's location or as agreed upon during the coordination process. The app encourages prompt pickup to minimize food waste.

• **Feedback and Ratings:** Both donors and recipients have the option to provide feedback and ratings based on their experience. This helps maintain accountability and improve the overall user experience.

• **Community Engagement:** The Feed It Forward app also fosters community engagement by providing resources, educational content, and opportunities for users to get involved in food-related initiatives and events.

- **Continuous Improvement:** The app's developers regularly update and improve its features based on user feedback, technological advancements, and emerging trends in the fight against food waste and hunger.

The Feed It Forward app serves as a bridge between those who have excess food and those who are in need, facilitating the redistribution of surplus food and reducing food waste. By leveraging technology and the power of community, the app strives to create a more sustainable and equitable food system.

Overcoming Challenges and Embracing Success

Developing a multilingual app comes with its own set of challenges. In this section, we uncover the obstacles faced by Chef Jagger Gordon and his team during the app's expansion. From technical complexities to cultural sensitivities, we explore how they navigated these hurdles and celebrated the success of making Feed It Forward available in multiple languages.

Supporting Ukraine

Chef Jagger Gordon's Ukrainian engagement holds a special place in his heart. This section focuses on his deep connection to Ukraine and his dedication to providing food relief during the country's challenging times.

We witness how the availability of the Feed It Forward app in Ukrainian has strengthened community ties and enabled more effective assistance to those affected by food insecurity in Ukraine.

Embracing the Spanish-Speaking World

The Feed It Forward app's expansion into languages like Spanish, opens the doors to a vast community affected by hunger across different countries. We explore the efforts made to adapt the app to Spanish-speaking regions, including collaborations with local organizations, translations, and culturally relevant approaches to food sharing.

Empowering Communities Through Technology

This section highlights the transformative power of technology in addressing food insecurity on a global scale. We examine how the multilingual Feed It Forward app has empowered individuals and communities, enabling them to share surplus food, access resources, and create lasting change in their local areas.

Amplifying Impact Through Collaboration

Chef Jagger Gordon understands the significance of collaboration in achieving lasting change. We highlight the partnerships formed with linguists, community leaders, and technology experts to ensure accurate translations and seamless user experiences across different language versions of the Feed It Forward app.

The Power of Unity

In the final section of this chapter, we reflect on the profound impact that language and unity can have in addressing global challenges such as childhood hunger. We explore the stories of individuals who have benefitted from *Feed It Forward's* work, demonstrating how the power of language can amplify and create a more equitable world.

A Global Movement

As we conclude this chapter, we embrace the significance of Chef Jagger Gordon's global mission, including the Feed It Forward app. We emphasize the importance of linguistic inclusivity and the potential of technology to unite individuals from different backgrounds in the fight against food waste and childhood hunger. With the app's expanded reach, we are reminded that compassion knows no language barriers and that together, we can build a more sustainable and nourished future for all.

Feed It Forward's innovative approach to addressing food waste and food insecurity has gained recognition and support from both the local community and beyond. Their initiatives provide practical solutions to tackle these issues while fostering a sense of dignity and community for those in need, which aims to provide food for those in need.

The program has gained global recognition, and Chef Jagger has received numerous awards for his philanthropic work, including being recognized as a global hero, community leader, and entrepreneur of the year.

Chef Jagger Gordon's achievements extend beyond his philanthropy. He is also an award-winning international best-selling author, editor-in-chief of *OutdoorLifestyle Magazine* and a Guinness World Record participant*.

His culinary expertise and passion for cooking have led him to teach culinary classes, including molecular gastronomic techniques and some of the world's best cuisines. His skills and dedication have earned him appearances on national television, where he showcases his talent and spreads awareness about food insecurity.

In an extraordinary display of courage and selflessness, Chef Jagger has used his military training to take his program to war-torn Ukraine to assist those struggling with food security. He and his elite team face grave dangers, including being shot at and targeted by bombs. They continue to cook and provide meals while risking their lives to make a difference in the lives of others.

In addition to his humanitarian efforts, Chef Jagger Gordon plans to create a documentary series highlighting his global endeavours. This series will showcase his team's presence during natural disasters and their unwavering commitment to helping those in need internationally. Through his travels around the world, Chef Jagger also aims to learn new cuisines and expand his culinary knowledge to all through his technological advancement and presents through all media platforms.

Stay Tuned as there are always new exciting adventures from Chef Jagger Sean Gordon.

Conclusion

Chef Jagger Gordon's story is one of remarkable resilience, compassion, and determination. He has become a beacon of hope for those facing food insecurity, demonstrating that even in the face of adversity, one person can make a significant difference in the lives of others.

If you would like to support our mission, you can make a monetary donation now.

https://feeditforward.ca/
Info@feeditforward.ca
1-647-510-(CHEF)2433

For your chef's experience anywhere around the world, catering needs that support and fund *Feed It Forward's* initiatives, you can book direct now

https://cateringagency.ca/
 http://jaggergordon.com/
Jagger@feeditforward.ca
1-647-879-(TRY-CHEF)2433

Watch all the adventures on Instagram and or our YouTube channel.

https://www.instagram.com/chefjaggergordon/?hl=en

https://youtube.com/@feeditforward5192

All Your Outdoor creations!
http://www.outdoorlifestylemagazine.com/

* https://www.guinnessworldrecords.com/world-records/most-authors-signing-the-same- book-simultaneously

Jagger S Gordon

Editor In Chief,
Outdoor Lifestyle Magazine
Executive Chef,
Jagger Gordon Catering/Consulting
Blazing Kitchen
Souvlaki Hut
Flame
Soup Bar
Feed The Future
Founder/ CEO,
Feed It Forward.ca
Outdoorlifestylemagazine.com

•

International Bestselling Author X 3
Guinness Book Of World Records participant
Awarded Global Hero and Urban Hero
•For general inquiries on food rescue please email
info@feeditforward.com
•For catering or consulting inquiries, please email
Jagger@feeditforward.ca
•For all media and OLMag content please email
jagger@outdoorlifestylemagazine.com

--

Don't forget to download Feed It Forward Free Food App

MASTERING SALES — THE FINAL REQUIRED ELEMENT

Susan Postnikoff

Sales Tactics and Strategies

There are hundreds of books and training programs about sales strategies and tactics, sales psychology, prospecting, presenting, pitching, and closing. There are books on keywords and phrases and types of questioning techniques, and there are books that highlight the importance of listening, being authentic, connecting, building relationships, and building trust. But very few sales training books or programs can help you be your authentic self as you engage your buyer in a deeply meaningful sales conversation.

Authenticity, Trust, and Ethics

Being truly authentic means coming from a place of honesty and integrity where you truly believe in the product or service that you are tasked with selling and do so from a place of servitude. With the true goal of a mutually beneficial transaction, you offer to enroll your customer into purchasing a product and/or service that will truly benefit them. Building repeat and referral business is the greatest form of advertising one can ever hope for, and that means that you must ensure you are matching your offering to the needs of your customer.

You may get pats on the back and a commission cheque for making an impossible sale by using your powers of persuasion and mastery of tactics and strategies; but what does this do for your credibility? How might this impact your future with this and other clients? There are a lot of great products and services, and it is usually possible to match them with the right buyer. If you don't believe that is true, then you may want to find a different product or service to sell. How we show up for others – how we are perceived by those that matter to us – creates our identity. The words of others about us in our jobs, our careers and our industries shape our identity and determine our successes and failures. We need to ensure that we are trusted and deserving of that trust as we build relationships with clients and coworkers that will establish our ultimate potential. Every time we chip away at that trust and perpetrate on our ethics, we lower our self-identity and our career identity. The result is a loss of self-confidence, a loss of trust and diminishing opportunities.

Often, a sales representative has an image of someone that they look up to or even an image of how they perceive themselves, which they try to portray as they deliver their sales presentations. This results in the rep presenting behind an invisible mask that causes them to use words, intonation, or body language that is not congruent with their authentic inner being. The consequence is a lack of connection that neither they nor their customer can pinpoint. It just feels a little off, and the full potential for trust is not realized.

Adjusting to Changes in the Market

There are situations where a salesperson has difficulty presenting authentically or meeting sales targets because of some deficiency in the product or service provided. This often happens because our world is very dynamic, and systems, technologies and products are being designed and created at faster and faster rates. Product manufacturers and service providers are tasked with the need to grow and change and stay ahead of the curve. As a sales representative, there will inevitably be times when a product or system currently being sold starts to lose its appeal to the customer and may be obsolete before the next generation is available. Sometimes the pressure to meet sales quotas or to maintain one's income can cause a sales professional to make a sale that is not really in the client's best interest. There can, at times, be a fine line between selling a tried-and-true gold standard, and recognizing when it is no longer of true value to the customer.

Rather than breach ethics to meet targets, it is a much higher level of performance to take honest feedback to our executive teams and to hold conversations with our customers about how we can better meet their needs. As much as we may have spent time in the past selling our customers on our previous and current offering, there may come a time when we need to sell our team and our employer on the necessity to adjust course and create new products and systems.

If you are not able to successfully engage your current management team in making the necessary adjustments, then it may be time for a change. The universe might be letting you know it's time to move on and either find a new job or create a new business. And, if you can engage your executive team, you may have just opened a whole new world of opportunity for yourself while also serving the best interests of your employer and your clients.

Listening

Listening is a word that has been getting more and more attention when it comes to sales. We have pretty much all evolved from the days of pitching features and benefits and then asking for orders. Our pitches have been integrated with sales strategies and techniques to draw information from our prospective buyers.

From planning to prospecting to closing, we have incorporated tactics and strategies that involve asking specific open-ended questions and listening for answers. Most sales professionals now have plans and pitches, and scripted processes. Some of them are very well constructed! And some sales professionals use them with grace and ease for the good of both their own company and their clients' businesses.

Most of these sales systems are designed to help the seller guide a qualified buyer down the path of understanding how the product or service will truly be of great value to the buyer and is, therefore, worth the investment, followed, of course, by a final negotiation on price and a finalizing of the formal sales contract.

For several reasons – perhaps lack of confidence, lack of experience or product knowledge, or just not being able to connect authentically — there are those sales professionals that do not effectively listen or connect.

Many people confuse the process of listening with the physiological act of hearing. Some sales professionals are so engrossed in the tactics and strategies that they are being run by them rather than using them as a guide.

I think the greatest listening mistake sales professionals make is that rather than wholly and authentically listening for the message the customer is trying to deliver, they instead target their hearing for specific words or phrases that will trigger the next step in the pitch deck.

The Role Interpretation in Listening Plays

Any sales professional that believes in the product or service they represent will be able to harness the ability to connect authentically and to listen for the intended message rather than keywords or phrases. This ability does not come from reading a sales book. This type of learning comes from becoming comfortable with oneself, through self-reflection, and through an exploration of how one interprets information they receive.

The truth about hearing and listening is that beyond the physiological process, we all tend to filter the information we receive through our past experiences, culture, and social influences. We all interpret information differently based on our individuality. No two people – not even identical twins raised by the same set of parents — share the exact same experiences and perspectives.

The need to be more present and connected with our clients becomes exceptionally clear when we understand that we are each – including our customers – interpreting information through a unique set of filters. These filters are virtually unlimited and include our religion, gender, race, family life, friends, education, life experiences and perhaps even our very own genetic mix of DNA. It is with this understanding that we need to start becoming better observers of ourselves and of those whom we interact with.

When we are with our families, we likely have more similarities than differences. But in sales, we encounter customers that come from very different situations and backgrounds. I have heard many people in the past make the declaration, *"Anyone would have made the same decision as me in that situation!"* But that simply is not true.

When we develop enough self-awareness to see ourselves through the eyes of others and even more deeply through the filters and interpretations of others, then we can truly listen authentically to the message being communicated.

The Final Element for Mastering Sales

This ability to observe and understand the filters through which we each interpret information is the final element that creates masters in the art of sales. To be a sales professional, we do need to plan our sales strategies and tactics, prospect effectively, ask the right questions at the right time, etc. And most importantly, we need to develop an acute awareness of how we and those we are communicating with may be interpreting the information being communicated.

First, as a listener/receiver and sender/speaker of communication, we can explore our own filters and interpretations. Second, we listen acutely to messages we receive from our customer, and pay attention to the filters and interpretations that may have affected what they said to us. Third, we listen for our listener's listening and interpretation as we speak to them. With commitment to this practice, we will develop the ability to be in a conversation and simultaneously observe all the possible filters and interpretations affecting the communication between ourselves and our clients.

This practice ultimately enables us to alter the course of our conversation or pitch as needed, to ask for or provide clarification when appropriate, and to determine the best possible products or services we can offer to meet the prospective buyer's true needs.

By practicing this element of communication, we will be speaking directly into our buyer's listening as we address objections and concerns and pave the path for the buyer to close themselves on the products and services presented that best serve their needs.

This final element of understanding and observing filtering and interpretation is how we achieve true Mastery as a Sales Professional and allow our buyers to talk themselves into placing the order.

Susan Postnikoff

Susan grew up on a farm in Saskatchewan, Canada, and moved to Toronto to complete her Bachelor of Science in Physical Education. Upon graduating from university, she took a management contract with the Metropolitan Toronto Housing Authority as the manager of the Aquatics Department with 27 swimming pools in subsidized housing projects. At MTHA, she was given the task of reviewing a 4-inch-thick management consulting assessment and preparing a formal and concise report to advise the Executive Council of MTHA on recommendations for the aquatic facilities, staffing and recreational offerings. Susan's analysis, research and recommendations resulted in more than $100,000 in annual budget savings for the department while increasing the motivation and cohesion of staff and the safety of the facilities. It was a very rewarding endeavour, and it highlighted her natural analytic abilities.

After a few years, Susan left recreation management and started her medical device sales career. She worked for a spine implant manufacturer called Danek and was immersed in an industry with technologies that were transforming medical procedures and enhancing patients' lives. In 2001, Medtronic purchased Danek, and Susan moved to California to work for Medtronic Sofamor Danek (MSD). Prior to moving to California, she had chalked up four consecutive years of exceptional sales growth – from 1997 to 2001, her sales increases were 52%, 109%, 44% and 128%. In the USA, she received recognition as "The Best of the Best" for initial sales of the disruptive stem cell technology, Bone Morphogenetic Protein-2. In 2003 Susan began working with medical device startups as Regional Sales Manager and then as Area Sales Director. She put her analytic skills to work once again, creating line-item forecasts, business plans, strategic marketing plans and training programs. Susan authored compliance training courses and manuals for sales representatives working in the hospital environment and was a speaker at multiple educational conferences, including the 2005 American Academy of Orthopedic Surgery Annual Meeting.

As a beach volleyball enthusiast, Susan has coached high school and club teams and has played in FIVB and AVP Professional Beach Volleyball Tournaments. Susan is certified by the National Coaching Certification Program for Level 2 Theory of Coaching and is an NASM Corrective Exercise Specialist. She also studied NLP and became a Certified Master Hypnotist and Hypnotherapist. Susan has provided career transition coaching, relationship coaching, sales and customer service training, and has consulted on sales and operations integration and corporate culture shift.

GOD ALLOWS SUCH EVENTS TO OCCUR
Katherine Kovin-Pacino

I appreciate the opportunity to introduce myself. I am Katherin Kovin-Pacino, a renowned American actress and bestselling co-author. With a strong lineage tracing back to the Daughters of the American Revolution (DAR), an esteemed organization honoring the contributions of women in early American history, my roots are deeply intertwined with the spirit of independence, education, and patriotism.

Additionally, my maternal grandmother, Kate Penland, was married to my biological grandfather, George B. Patton, a distinguished jurist and former Attorney General of North Carolina. These familial ties, along with my passion for patriotism and politics, have shaped my journey.

While Al Pacino, my stepson and a celebrated actor, has often taken the spotlight, I have carved my own path in the industry. I have had the privilege of appearing in more than 15 high-budget films, including the upcoming *"Death Realm,"* produced by Rayster Michaels and Eric Zuley, and *"Who's Gonna Take Care of Me?"* directed by Marneen Lynne Fields, a renowned stunt actress turned producer/director.

I would like to express my heartfelt gratitude to my dear friend, Robert J Moore, for giving me the opportunity to contribute to this remarkable book. Robert's inspiring career and resilience in the face of challenges have touched the lives of many. Currently, he is embarking on two noteworthy film projects: *"Reinventing Freedom,"* a documentary about his own life, and "*Resilience*," a true story that captures his remarkable journey. I am immensely proud of him.

In recent times, we have witnessed a growing desire among certain individuals to dismantle statues and architectural elements they deem offensive, driven by their own specific mindset. Many secretly wish to rewrite history to further their personal agendas.

However, I strongly believe that these statues should remain untouched as they are vital reminders of our history. They serve as constant reminders of past atrocities, prompting us to declare, "*Never again.*" It is crucial not to forget the blatant errors and embarrassing moments they represent. We must acknowledge that power, money, and mass control are often at stake in these discussions.

The question of why God allows such events to occur delves into the concept of polarity within the Universe. On Earth, we exist as students in a school where our purpose is to learn valuable lessons. I firmly believe that each of us has a soul contract that guides us in handling challenges with integrity, choosing the path of righteousness, and helping others find their way toward a brighter future for the collective good.

Polarity manifests itself through the stark contrasts of good versus bad, freedom versus enslavement, and the divisions between the elite and the common. By navigating and understanding these polarities, we not only grow individually but also acquire the wisdom to impart to others.

As Americans, we are incredibly fortunate to have a Constitution and a Bill of Rights that set our country apart. We must not allow these precious gifts to be stolen from us under any circumstances.

There are leaders who, disguising their actions as serving the people's interests, attempt to erode our rights, one amendment at a time, for their personal gain, power, or agendas. It is essential to remember the importance of unity. As the adage goes, "*United we stand, divided we fall.*"

I take great pride in being an American, and I am unwavering in my commitment to fight for our God-given rights, regardless of the consequences. This is the path our ancestors would have wanted for us. I hold onto the hope that we can fulfill the original vision of America as "America the Beautiful," the "Land of the Free," and the "Home of the Brave."

Although we are far from perfect, we must learn from past mistakes to ensure our efforts are not in vain. We owe this to our children and grandchildren, who represent our future. Putting my trust in God, I firmly believe that we can protect ourselves from divisive agendas, such as those outlined in Saul Alinsky's "*Rules for Radicals*," which seek to dismantle the foundations of our country and families. These agendas do not align with our civil liberties and, truth be told, are part of a "Communist/Marxist" strategy of "divide and conquer."

"United we stand, divided we fall" holds true not just for America but for any nation. I gladly pledge to defend my country today and always, as I am proud to be an American. May God bless the USA!

In the words of singer Lee Greenwood, "*I am grateful to be living in a time where the flag still symbolizes freedom that cannot be taken away.*"

A COLLABORATIVE JOURNEY THROUGH TRAUMA TO SUCCESS

Sheila Jones

Reflecting on my life, I never stopped to "sum up" my accomplishments or acknowledge the transformational moments. However, in 2020 I was in a boating accident and nearly lost my foot. My doctor walked into my room and said, "You probably will never walk again on your two feet." At that moment, my future goals flashed before my eyes. I sought out mental health assistance to better manage the emotional impacts of this injury. In a moment of self-discovery, unknowingly, my life comprised of setting goals, overcoming obstacles, and achieving success both professionally and personally. My life was a series of transformations.

My professional life began at Busch's Chesapeake Inn. I arrived with zero skill sets, a desire to learn, and a resolute work ethic. I held a series of progressively challenging jobs that resulted in being crowned FRY COOK!

My passion was partnered with a desire to learn and grow. I sought out great teachers, requested feedback on my recipes and designed intriguing plate presentations. I studied food and recipes at the local bookstore, and my career moved forward. I was hired at the Sheraton Hotel on the outskirts of Washington, DC, as a line cook. Our Sous Chef was very professional and demanding. For example, he gave culinary pop quizzes nightly and critiqued each plate. I respected him. I learned a great deal and grew from his teaching methods.

Over the years, I continued to strive for perfection. I set my sights on a position with Northwoods in Annapolis, MD, an award-winning food and wine restaurant with stellar service. Every chef was a graduate of The Culinary Institute of America, in which I was not. I was self-taught. I secured the position of salad and appetizer maker – a triumphant career moment. I developed recipes, continued studying, testing, and seeking feedback. I pushed myself and eventually became a chef at Northwoods.

Although I was successful at Northwoods, I sought out a different challenge - a personal and professional growth goal. I focused on obtaining a Food Science Degree, which I attained in 12 years, and the next chapter of my career began to unfold.

In September of 1999, I launched my career in Corporate America – I was hired as the Application Chef for the Nestle-Food Service division. This transformational moment was laced with emotions of fear, excitement, and self-doubt.

I relocated to New Milford, CT and worked in the Nestle culinary headquarters. Although the physical space looked the same as my previous restaurant kitchens with stoves and frying pans, I was now working in a test kitchen where I was challenged to master the application methods for over 400 different ingredients. I was struggling to create recipes and, at times, questioned my decision as to why I left the comfort of the restaurant business where my success had grown easily. However, despite doubts, I continued to seek success in this new professional world. After working for months developing recipes in partnership with an international customer, we sold a recipe worth $ 1 million dollars that was available in every major grocery store in America. With this major milestone, my confidence grew.

I continued to seek opportunities to grow both professionally and personally. I left Nestle for an opportunity at Campbell Soup Company. I began my career at Campbell's as part of the innovation team and exercised my skills in food science and culinary arts. Innovation was particularly challenging as our job was to create new food products, and we failed more times than we succeeded.

Dimensionally my responsibilities increased, and I accepted a position with Campbell's internship team. My role included mentoring, coaching, and creating career development plans for interns.

In my personal life, I volunteered in my community for a job rehabilitation program called Respond Culinary which provided culinary training for formerly incarcerated men. Personally, this was a profound moment of learning and growth. As I worked with the men, my desire to contribute increased. This, along with my professional growth, inspired me to seek a career move.

My employment confidentiality agreement with my previous employer Campbell's restricted my ability to accept positions in product development. As a result, I joined Walmart as a Senior Quality System Manager. I was placed in the produce division and was assigned to California's agriculture fields. A new world of learning, challenges, and obstacles lay ahead, and I felt vulnerable. I collaborated with the growers to increase my knowledge and formed incredible relationships that remain intact today.

I accepted an opportunity to become the Director of Product Development for the Consumable and Health and Wellness division. This acknowledged my unique skill set beyond developing food in a kitchen and allowed the application of my abilities across a portfolio of products, including diabetic meters, incontinence products, pet food, drugs, supplements, and other consumable items.

Together as a team, we built a successful business division, and served our company and customers. During my time at Walmart, I intentionally broadened my store operations knowledge by working in 15 different departments.

Further, I met ophthalmologists and pharmacists and gained significant retail operations knowledge. In the corporate offices, I would dedicate five hours a month to meeting with cross-functional leaders from different divisions, such as apparel, home entertainment, toys, and tire centers, to further learn the business.

Personally, I dedicated myself to expanding my communication skills. I read books, studied TEDx talks, and practiced public speaking. I completed multiple in-depth executive presentation programs that focused on content development, body language, voice inflection, and hand gestures. I was routinely videotaped and received feedback from my peers and mentors. Over and over, I worked to improve my presentation skills. I was relentless!

I continued progressing towards my personal goals, became a mentor, and partnered with executive leadership teams to create signature programs for promotability, relationship development and embracing the Walmart culture. I led our employment engagement survey and action plans and built succession planning for our division.

I continued my personal development, and I started writing. I was convinced I could write a book. After a few months, I went from being excited to ignoring the editor check-ins. I made excuses. I was stuck, scared, and did not seek help. I had hit my growth wall.

After a fishing trip, I was inspired to write a children's book. At Barnes and Noble, on Saturdays, I studied book sizes, palette colors, word choice, character design and development. I could feel my energy increasing and my excitement brewing. One Friday night, on my way home from work, I purchased 21 – 2'x2' whiteboards. I worked through the night and created the first draft of *Amir's Big Catch*. For the next two years, I persevered and collaborated with an incredibly talented team of professionals. Together, we won a gold medal. I was officially an award-winning children's book author, *Amir's Big Catch* and it is available on Amazon.com. What did I learn from this experience – collaboration.

I was recruited to join Advanced Food Products, a subsidiary of Savencia Fromage and Dairy, in New Holland, PA. The goal was to grow the company. Many days the objective seemed impossible; however, I was determined to achieve success.

I launched a sequence of activities, including strategy setting, changing the culture, hiring talent, and mobilizing our workforce. Some days were just tough and exhausting. Maintaining the right momentum and energy level was critical.

I built a continuous improvement mindset that consisted of a cycle of work, win, celebrate and repeat, and in the process, we achieved small gains that accumulated into big wins. After three years, I was promoted to the executive leadership team, and in the end, delivered incredible growth.

My personal life continued to expand, and I became a board member for Vets2Industry. I mentored 1000s of veterans. However, I was getting restless. While hiking deep in the woods of Lancaster, PA, I asked myself, "What could I create that will impact people at a greater level?" I set a personal challenge and goal to help 250 thousand people reach their personal and professional goals.

In pursuit of this goal, my personal life was interrupted by my foot injury. As I lay in bed questioning my future, I was invited to join a Yoga Teacher Training - question and answer meeting. At that moment, I became acutely aware that I needed this training. I started my yoga training restricted to bed poses. Over time I physically healed. Yoga profoundly changed my perspective and relationship with my mind and body. The yoga training unlocked a new level of what could be achieved with intentional action and commitment to a goal. I graduated as a certified Yoga instructor and continue to practice every day.

Immediately after obtaining my Yoga certification, I reignited my goal of helping 250 thousand people grow and develop. I became a Maxwell Leadership Certified Team Member and a Maxwell DISC Certified Behavioral Consultant.

I left my comfortable corporate position and started Whicked Results, a challenge of epic portion. We are highly skilled in three areas – coaching, speaking, and training. We apply this knowledge to businesses, people, and education. Our business includes job and career coaching, ranging from interns to CEOs.

Additionally, we coach and train speakers to deliver TEDx talks. Furthermore, we focus on serving teachers, principals, and administrators to achieve success through classroom management and inspire students' education through engagement and motivational training in schools.

In reflection, my professional and personal life is a sum of continual movement to seek more. I have reinvented and transformed myself numerous times.

As a result, I continue to ask myself what do I need to do, what do I need to learn, and who do I need to work with as I seek to impact and contribute on a bigger stage.

I have learned in a profound way that life is short, and in an instant, your life can change.

I am committed to reaching my goal to help 250 thousand people grow and develop. I am confident that I was meant to collaborate with the world!

Sheila Jones

Sheila Jones is a Business Executive and CEO of *Whicked Results*. She is a Maxwell Leadership Certified Team Member and Maxwell DISC Certified Behavioral Consultant. She is a Coach, Speaker, and Trainer. She is a personal and professional development coach. She is the Head Speaker Coach for TEDx York Beach, Maine. Her successes include preparing the speakers to present at the TEDx event; some have achieved the prestigious Editor's Pick Status. Additionally, Sheila is certified in educational programs for classroom management and student engagement and motivation taught in school districts. Sheila has held leadership positions with Nestle, Campbell Soup, Walmart and Savencia Fromage and Dairy and was responsible for leading billion-dollar business divisions. Additionally, she is a contributing author for Emerging Leaders Magazine and is an award-winning children's book author.

Feel free to continue the conversation via email: sheila@whickedresults.com

www.ingramcontent.com/pod-product-compliance
Lightning Source LLC
Chambersburg PA
CBHW031526120626
46545CB00005B/2024